THE **MINI** ROUGH GUIDE TO
NEW YORK

ROUGH
GUIDES

R TAILOR-MADE TRIP
STARTS HERE

...de trips and unique adventures crafted by local experts

...ugh Guides has been inspiring travellers for more than ...years. Leave it to our local experts to create your perfect itinerary and book it at local rates.

Don't follow the crowd – find your own path.

HOW ROUGHGUIDES.COM/TRIPS WORKS

STEP 1 Pick your dream destination, tell us what you want and submit an enquiry.

STEP 2 Fill in a short form to tell your local expert about your dream trip and preferences.

STEP 3 Our local expert will craft your tailor-made itinerary. You'll be able to tweak and refine it until you're completely satisfied.

STEP 4 Book online with ease, pack your bags and enjoy the trip! Our local expert will be on hand 24/7 while you're on the road.

PLAN AND BOOK YOUR TRIP AT
ROUGHGUIDES.COM/TRIPS

HOW TO DOWNLOAD YOUR FREE EBOOK

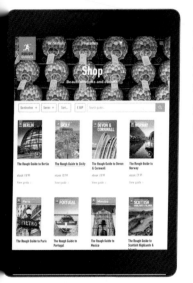

1. Visit **www.roughguides.com/free-ebook** or scan the **QR code** below

2. Enter the code **newyork379**

3. Follow the simple step-by-step instructions

For troubleshooting contact: mail@roughguides.com

10 THINGS NOT TO MISS

1. **BROOKLYN BRIDGE**
   Stroll across this 19th-century icon. See page 33.

2. **THE GUGGENHEIM**
   As well known for its architecture as for its paintings. See page 53.

3. **STATUE OF LIBERTY**
   Welcoming millions to New York since its dedication in 1886. See page 28.

4. **MOMA**
   Home to one of the world's best collections of modern art. See page 42.

5. **TIMES SQUARE**
   Get up close to the spectacle of this iconic world landmark. See page 34.

6. **EMPIRE STATE BUILDING**
   The famed skyscraper offers eye-popping views of Manhattan. See page 46.

7. **AMERICAN MUSEUM OF NATURAL HISTORY**
   From dinosaurs to planets, it's all here. See page 62.

8. **GREENWICH VILLAGE**
   A laid-back feel characterizes the infamously bohemian 'Village'. See page 73.

9. **THE METROPOLITAN MUSEUM OF ART**
   A vast and fabulous trove of historical treasures. See page 51.

10. **CENTRAL PARK**
    Unwind in New York's playground. See page 55.

A PERFECT DAY

9.00am

Breakfast. Enjoy the quintessential breakfast of New Yorkers – bagel, lox, and cream cheese – at Katz's Delicatessen on the Lower East Side. After breakfast, stroll down Ludlow where you can window-shop the hip neighborhood's boutiques.

10.15am

Lower East Side origins. Just a couple of doors down from Delancey on Orchard Street is the Lower East Side Tenement Museum. Here you can step back in time and learn about the immigrants who originally populated the Lower East Side with a visit to the tenement building built in 1863. You can tour recreated homes of former residents who lived here between the 1860s and 1980s.

11.15am

Walk to Brooklyn. Continue heading south, through bustling Chinatown, to the Brooklyn Bridge entrance at the end of Centre Street. Cross the bridge via the walkway to arrive in Brooklyn at the other side of the East River. It takes around a half hour to cross the bridge, or a little more if you stop to take in the view.

12.30pm

Pizza perfect. A Brooklyn institution, Grimaldi's Pizzeria (1 Front Street; exit the bridge via the first stairs) is a must. After lunch, wander down Old Fulton Street. Grab an ice cream from Ample Hills Creamery (1 Water Street) before strolling the promenade along the East River in Brooklyn Bridge Park. The views of lower Manhattan are picture-perfect.

N NEW YORK

2.30pm

Old Masters in the afternoon. Take the subway to the Upper East Side. The temporary Frick Madison (945 Madison Avenue at 75th Street) is a wonderful museum, much more manageable than the nearby Met. The collection includes works by artists including Rembrandt, Vermeer and Gainsborough. Note that the collection should move back to its original home, the mansion of Henry Frick, at the end of 2023/early 2024.

4.30pm

Central Park. After the Frick, take a walk through Central Park, which is just across Fifth Avenue. There is an entrance at 72nd and Fifth Avenue. Stroll to the Lake, Strawberry Fields or the Shakespeare Garden.

6.30pm

Dinner time. Head to one of the best steakhouses in the Times Square neighborhood, Charlie Palmer Steak NYC, for the pre-theater prix-fixe menu. Or try the legendary Sardi's in the heart of New York's Theater District for dinner and a pre-show cocktail.

8.00pm

Broadway. Hit the Great White Way and enjoy one of the many Broadway or off-Broadway performances.

10.30pm

City lights. Top off your day with a perfect panoramic view of the city with all its sparkling lights from Top of the Rock on the 69th floor of the Rockefeller Center. Or head to the on-site bar, Bar SixtyFive, for cocktails with a view.

CONTENTS

OVERVIEW   `10`

HISTORY AND CULTURE   `13`

OUT AND ABOUT   `23`

Downtown   24
One World Trade Center and 9/11 Memorial 24; Battery Park City 25; Statue of Liberty and Ellis Island 27; Fraunces Tavern 30; Wall Street 31; Brooklyn Bridge 32; South Street Seaport 33

West Midtown – Theater District   34
Times Square and Broadway 34; North of Times Square 35; West 42nd Street 36

Central Midtown   37
Bryant Park 37; Rockefeller Center 38; Fifth Avenue 40; Museum of Modern Art 42

East Midtown   43
Madison and Park Avenues 43; Grand Central and the Chrysler Building 44; United Nations 45

South Midtown   46
Empire State Building 46

Upper East Side – The Museum Mile   49
Frick Madison 50; Metropolitan Museum of Art 51; Neue Galerie 53; Guggenheim Museum 53; Other museums 54

Central Park   55
Park highlights 57

Upper West Side   59
Lincoln Center 60; Natural History Museum 62; Columbia University Area 64

Harlem and North Manhattan   65
An historic district 66; Washington Heights 68; The Cloisters 68

Other neighborhoods   69
The Lower East Side 69; The Bowery and Nolita 70; Chinatown 71; Little Italy 72; SoHo and Tribeca 72; Greenwich Village 73; East Village 75; Meatpacking District and Chelsea 76

Excursions to the outer boroughs 79

Brooklyn 79; The Bronx 80; Queens 82

THINGS TO DO 85

FOOD AND DRINK 99

TRAVEL ESSENTIALS 115

WHERE TO STAY 132

INDEX 139

HIGHLIGHTS

The 9/11 effect 10

Skyscrapers 18

Important Dates 21

Icon of hope 24

Liberty Science Center 28

Broadway 34

CityPass 49

Harlem's churches 66

Village voices 77

Museum shops 88

Discount theater tickets 90

New York from the water 96

What's on 98

Food Halls 100

Brunch 102

A NOTE TO READERS

At Rough Guides, we always strive to bring you the most up-to-date information. This book was produced during a period of continuing uncertainty caused by the Covid-19 pandemic, so please note that content is more subject to change than usual. We recommend checking the latest restrictions and official guidance.

OVERVIEW

'The city'

New Yorkers refer to Manhattan as 'the city', even though they identify the other boroughs by name. For addresses, 'New York, New York' means Manhattan.

First-time visitors to New York usually come with wide eyes and high expectations. The quintessential urban landscape – the Big Apple – does not disappoint. No matter what it is you are after, you will find it: great theater, marvelous museums, luxurious hotels, fascinating history, exciting nightlife, sumptuous dining. Peace and quiet can even be found, in the rooms of high-rise hotels far above the teeming streets, or by venturing into the upper reaches of Central Park, or walking out onto the terrace overlooking the Hudson River at the Cloisters.

At first, New York can be a little overwhelming, however once you get over the crowded streets and the wailing sirens, you can

THE 9/11 EFFECT

Every American over a certain age can tell you the story of where they were and what they were doing when President John Kennedy was assassinated on November 22, 1963. Now, every New Yorker can tell you where they were and what they were doing the morning of September 11, 2001 when two terrorist-hijacked planes hit the World Trade Center. The average New Yorker has emerged from the tragedy of September 11 feeling no less rushed and impatient about day-to-day life, but certainly less invincible and far more vulnerable. A visit to the National September 11 Memorial & Museum on the site of the former Ground Zero and the new One World Trade Center is a must for visitors who wish to pay their respects in person.

Grand Central is a Beaux-Arts masterpiece

start to see that there is more to New York than its tourist attractions and museums. It's a city with depth and lots more to explore.

A CITY TRANSFORMED

If anything characterizes New York today, it is how much the city has raised itself up from the darker days of the 1970s and 1980s. Crime has now dropped to levels New Yorkers had not seen since the early 1960s, and the city is generally clean and efficient. As a result, both tourists and business people flock here in ever-increasing record numbers every year (66.6 million visitors in 2019). Everything was put on hold during the Covid-19 pandemic in 2020, but now in 2022 things are rapidly returning to normal.

If you want to see an example of how the city can reinvent itself, just look at Times Square. Until the early 1990s, the 'square' was filled with pornographic theaters, adult bookstores, and abandoned buildings. The Port Authority bus terminal was filled with hustlers and touts, and 42nd Street was really not a place one wanted to be after dark. Today Times Square is still choked, but with new, high-profile office buildings and hotels, refurbished Broadway theaters, shiny entertainment complexes, and tens of thousands of tourists. The adult theaters and bookstores are long gone, and media giants like MTV have reclaimed the space along with well-attended attractions including Madame Tussaud's Wax Museum.

The French-inspired Bryant Park

Not that the story is uniformly positive. The New York area has some of the highest homelessness rates in the country, exacerbated by the Covid-19 pandemic. The disparity between the rich and the poor is greater than ever. Most of the new housing being built in the city will be affordable only to those with the highest incomes. Nevertheless, almost every New York neighborhood has a good story to tell.

A GORGEOUS MOSAIC

It is difficult for mere mortals to live in such a complicated, crowded, and expensive city, so people can easily lose their tempers. But, for a place as large and diverse as New York City, everyone gets along pretty well. The five boroughs – Manhattan, Brooklyn, Queens, the Bronx, and Staten Island – have a total population of around 8.5 million. Brooklyn is the most populous, and Brooklyn and Queens each have more residents than Manhattan.

As a hub for immigration since colonial days, New York has always welcomed the world. Today people still arrive in large numbers, searching for wealth, happiness, freedom, or just a job, making the mixture even richer.

By the end of their first trip to New York, most visitors are hooked. Nothing is quite as exhilarating as walking the crowded streets of Midtown for the first time, or encountering works of art you've only read about in books.

HISTORY AND CULTURE

In 1524 Giovanni da Verrazano, a Florentine in the service of France, discovered what is now called New York Harbor. However, it would be a hundred years before the first settlers came to the area. Today the entrance to the harbor (the Verrazano Narrows) and the bridge across it are named after him.

NEW AMSTERDAM

Excitement finally began to build over the region's possibilities in 1609, after the Englishman Henry Hudson, working for the Dutch East India Company, sailed up what is now the Hudson River to Albany. In 1624, the new Dutch West India Company sent the first settlers to what is now Lower Manhattan. The following spring the colonists built a small town at the site, calling it New Amsterdam. The first two Dutch governors of the territory, Peter Minuit and Peter Stuyvesant, oversaw the development of a lively trading post. According to a popular city creation myth, it was Peter Minuit who in 1626 purchased the entire island of Manhattan from Native Americans for the equivalent of $24 in beads and cloth, at the site of present-day Bowling Green.

From the beginning, New Amsterdam was the most cosmopolitan center in the New World. The earliest immigrants included Walloons, Scandinavians, Germans, Spaniards, and Portuguese Jews, not to mention black slaves from the Caribbean. In 1643 a priest counted 18 languages spoken in this town of 1,500 inhabitants. An atmosphere of religious tolerance even attracted British dissidents from New England.

In 1653 Governor Peter Stuyvesant built a wall across the expanse of the island (at present-day Wall Street) in an effort to protect the Dutch settlers from the British, who had settled much

Map of New Amsterdam from 1660

of the area around New Amsterdam. But the effort was unnecessary. Unable or unwilling to put up a fight, the Dutch settlers surrendered to an English fleet on September 8, 1664. King Charles II gave the colony to his brother, the Duke of York, and New Amsterdam was re-christened New York.

NEW YORK

Although the city again came under Dutch control in 1673 (again without a fight) and was briefly known as New Orange, a treaty the following year returned it to British control. In the 18th century the town grew into a city of 25,000 and life became more comfortable. A city hall and several churches were built, and New York saw the foundation of King's College (today's Columbia University) as well as the creation of its first newspaper. Little of this era remains today. St. Paul's Chapel, built in 1766, is the oldest remaining church in New York. The Morris-Jumel mansion in Harlem also dates from this time.

British control of the colony of New York was a mixed success. Anti-British sentiment started early. In 1735 John Peter Zenger, publisher of the anti-government *New-York Weekly Journal*, was acquitted on charges of slander, an early victory for freedom of the press. (You can read more about the history of this victory at Federal Hall National Memorial in Lower Manhattan.) The city was split between loyalists to the crown and pro-independence 'patriots'. On June 27, 1775, half the town went to cheer George

Washington as he left to take command of the Continental Army in Boston, while the other half were down at the harbor giving a rousing welcome to the English governor, who had just returned from London. Similarly, the New York delegates voted against an early version of the Declaration of Independence.

THE NEW REPUBLIC

New York remained a British stronghold throughout the Revolutionary War and only gave up after the final surrender in Virginia in 1781. Two years later England recognized the independence of the American colonies. Washington returned triumphantly to New York and bade farewell to his officers at Fraunces Tavern. He later became the country's first president, when the city was briefly the first capital of the new United States of America. Washington took the oath of office on the balcony of the original Federal Hall (formerly the New York City Hall), then went to pray at St. Paul's Chapel, where you can see his pew.

Although Philadelphia took over as the nation's political capital in 1790, New York remained America's commercial center. In 1800 (the same year Alexander Hamilton built the Grange, which is in today's Harlem), the population had reached 60,000 – twice what it had been ten years earlier.

The city was soon beset with housing shortages and sanitation problems. In the heat of summer, when disease and epidemics were commonplace, the inhabitants would escape to their 'country' homes in such far-flung places as the village of Greenwich (now Greenwich Village) or the wilderness that became today's Upper East Side. In 1811 the state legislature came to the conclusion that any further growth of New York City must be regulated. The Randel Commission proposed that all new streets should only cross each other at right angles, with streets running east–west and avenues north–south. (Broadway was exempted.) The plan was immediately adopted, and as a result, everything above 14th Street is now a grid.

BURGEONING TOWN

When the Erie Canal opened in 1825, linking the Great Lakes to the Hudson River, New York became the ocean gateway for an immense hinterland. Business flourished and shipyards abounded in this major port. However, housing was still substandard, and most residents lived in crowded conditions. In December 1835 a fire destroyed the heart of the business district around Hanover and Pearl streets, including almost all that remained from the Dutch era. But the city recovered quickly from this calamity.

In 1853 the Crystal Palace of the first American World's Fair went up in present-day Bryant Park. That same year, the state legislature authorized the building of a great public space, Central Park; the architects, Calvert Vaux and Frederick Law Olmsted, were chosen five years later, the same year the Crystal Palace was destroyed by fire.

By 1860, the city's population had reached an unruly 800,000. Governing the city proved difficult, riots occasionally erupted, and crime was becoming a big problem. Rampant government corruption was also taking its toll. William Marcy Tweed ran New York City along with his cohorts in the Tammany Hall political organization. He managed to fleece the city of some $200 million. When 'Boss Tweed' was finally arrested in 1871, the city was in bad shape indeed.

New York neverthe-less once again proved its

Cemetery to park

Many of New York's parks were originally potter's fields, where indigent people were buried. Both Washington Square Park and Bryant Park started out with this function.

resilience and bounced back. The late 19th century and early 20th witnessed the city's most dramatic growth to date. Many of New York's existing magnificent buildings were built at this time. New York banks financed the construction of the railways that opened up the western lands, the expansion of mines and mills, and the development of the new petroleum and automobile industries. Huge fortunes were made by the Vanderbilts, Rockefellers, Morgans, Carnegies, and Fricks, among others. These tycoons amassed fabulous art collections and funded many of the philanthropic and cultural institutions that make New York what it is today, from the Metropolitan Museum and Metropolitan Opera to the Frick Collection and the Rockefeller Center.

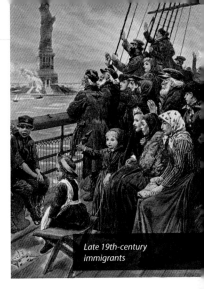

Late 19th-century immigrants

MASS IMMIGRATION

During the second half of the 19th century influxes of immigrants crowded into New York in search of a new and better life. The potato famine in Ireland and revolutionary ferment in Central Europe brought the Irish and Germans, who were soon followed by Italians, Poles, and Hungarians. The first important wave of Jews fleeing the pogroms of Russia and Eastern Europe arrived in the 1880s. Over 2 million newcomers landed in the city between 1885 and 1895, welcomed (after 1886) by the Statue of Liberty.

While the middle class moved to west-side neighborhoods near Central Park, the comfortable brownstone houses and mansions of the rich spread up Fifth Avenue and onto the east side. In 1870, construction started on a bridge to connect New York City with Brooklyn, a sizeable city in its own right. The invention of the elevator by Elisha Otis made it possible to construct 'skyscrapers' up to

SKYSCRAPERS

By the early 20th century, the development of 'steel skeleton' construction had finally made it possible to build tall. The first genuine skyscraper in New York was the **Flatiron Building**, erected in 1902 and with 22 stories. The **Equitable Building**, however, which appeared on Lower Broadway in 1916, was a 40-floor monster on an 'H'-shaped ground plan that filled an entire block. The walls were perpendicular, without any tiering, which plunged the whole neighborhood into shadow. The city was compelled to pass a 'zoning law', which stipulated that the upper floors of a skyscraper should be tiered to allow light through to the streets below. This resulted in the so-called 'wedding-cake' style of building, examples of which include the **Chrysler** and **Empire State Buildings** (1930 and 1931). Designed by Mies van der Rohe with Philip Johnson, and completed in 1958, the **Seagram Building** on Park Avenue was a simple tower with a straight facade, following the rules of the International Style. It overcame the zoning law by having a plaza at its base, setting the trend for later developments such as the Rockefeller Center.

Such a concentration of very tall buildings could never have been built without sturdy foundations, and the billion-year-old gneiss bedrock of Manhattan is as solid as it gets. Its closeness to the surface makes for relatively easy construction.

the amazing height of eight or ten stories.

In 1898, New York City (from then on known as Manhattan), Queens, Brooklyn, the Bronx, and Staten Island merged to form Greater New York, with a population of more than 3 million. After London, Greater New York was the world's most populous city.

The 9/11 Memorial

The early years of the 20th century witnessed further impressive growth. Genuine skyscrapers – including the Flatiron Building (1902) – were built, the first subway line opened (1904), and Manhattan and Brooklyn were linked by an under-river subway tunnel (1908). When the business boom finally burst in 1929, bread lines and jobless people became a common sight; a shantytown even sprang up in Central Park. In 1934, a dynamic Italian-born mayor named Fiorello La Guardia fought to introduce an important number of public-welfare measures and civic reform initiatives, which have characterized the city ever since.

HIGHS AND LOWS

After World War II, the United Nations set up its headquarters in New York on the banks of the East River, on land donated by the Rockefeller family. The 1950s saw phenomenal growth in the city but also economic downturn. New highways and cheaper cars and houses encouraged city-dwellers to move out to the suburbs. At the same time, in part because of this retreat, portions of the inner city began to decline. Even the beloved Brooklyn Dodgers moved to Los Angeles in 1958. True, Lincoln Center was built in the 1960s, and the World's Fair was held in Flushing Meadows, Queens, in 1964–65, but racial tensions also led to riots in Harlem, Bedford-Stuyvesant, and the South Bronx. The city reached a low point in 1975 when New York teetered on the edge of bankruptcy.

After mixed fortunes in the 1980s, when the city was known for its high crime rate, the 1990s brought better times. Things started looking up during the mayoralty of David Dinkins, the city's first black mayor, elected in 1989. But most of the improvements were not seen until the arrival of Rudolph Giuliani in 1993. A Republican mayor in a decidedly Democratic city, he brought order to the streets. After September 11, 2001, he took on the unexpected role as the public face of a city in turmoil. Mayor Michael Bloomberg, owner of the financial media empire that bears his name, succeeded him in January 2002. Over his three terms, Bloomberg launched public health initiatives (smoking and trans-fat bans), expanded bike lanes, and helped the city weather storms both literal (Hurricane Sandy) and figurative (the 2008 financial crisis).

New Yorkers continue to display their resilience in the face of repeated threats, adapting as necessary and getting on with their lives. The 9/11 Memorial opened 10 years after the devastation at Ground Zero with the connected museum opening in 2014.

In the same year, Bill de Blasio replaced Bloomberg as mayor, having run on a populist platform with an interest in addressing the economic inequality in the city. De Blasio's second term was marred by the Covid-19 epidemic that devastated the city in 2020 and 2021 – some 40,000 New Yorkers died from the virus. De Blasio was succeeded as mayor by fellow Democrat and ex-police officer Eric Adams in 2022, pledging to deal with growing concerns over crime and public safety in the wake of the epidemic.

IMPORTANT DATES

1609 Englishman Henry Hudson is the first European to step on to the island known to the local Algonquin Indians as Mannahatta.

1624 The Dutch West India Company establishes a settlement on the southern tip of Mannahatta, calling it New Amsterdam.

1664 War between England and Holland. New Amsterdam surrenders and is renamed New York after the Duke of York.

1776 The Revolutionary War begins; the colonies declare independence. British troops occupy New York until 1783.

1785–90 New York is capital of the new United States of America.

1830 Irish and German immigrants begin arriving in great numbers.

1835 Part of Manhattan is ravaged by the 'Great Fire.'

1861–5 American Civil War. Draft riots in Five Points neighborhood.

1865 Italians, Jews, and Chinese begin arriving in large numbers.

1886 Statue of Liberty, a gift from France, is unveiled.

1892 Ellis Island becomes the entry point for immigrants.

1929 The Wall Street Crash, and the start of the Great Depression.

1933–45 Europeans take refuge in New York from Nazi persecution.

1941 The US enters World War II.

1973 The World Trade Center opens.

1990 David Dinkins becomes the city's first African-American mayor.

1993 Rudolph Giuliani voted in as mayor and gets 'tough on crime.'

2001 Terrorists crash two hijacked planes into the World Trade Center. The buildings collapse, killing close to 3,000 people.

2008 Wall Street finds itself at the center of the global financial crisis.

2011 9/11 Memorial opens. Occupy Wall Street protesters descend on Lower Manhattan.

2012 Hurricane Sandy causes major damage and flooding in New York City.

2014 Democrat Bill de Blasio is elected mayor of New York.

2020 The Covid-19 pandemic devastates New York, leading to lockdowns, multiple restaurant closures and the suspension of Broadway shows for over a year-and-a-half.

2022 Democrat Eric Adams is sworn in as Mayor of New York City.

Fall in the West Village

OUT AND ABOUT

While the majority of visitors to New York never leave Manhattan, there is more to the city than its most famous borough. Those who venture to Brooklyn, for example, will find a world-class art museum along with parks, gardens, and fascinating neighborhoods. One of the country's great zoos is located in the Bronx, near an equally notable attraction, the New York Botanical Garden. In Queens you will find MoMa PS1, the largest contemporary art museum in New York, a top-notch filmmaking museum and the Noguchi Museum celebrating the work of Japanese American artist Isamu Noguchi. Meanwhile, the journey to Staten Island is that borough's highlight, a ferry ride right by the Statue of Liberty, and best of all, it is free.

However, Manhattan is the focus of most visitors' attentions, with its wealth of sights and activities. Only 13.5 miles (22km) long and 2 miles (3.5km) wide, New York's most popular borough is what everyone calls 'the city.' Getting your bearings in this metropolis is remarkably easy thanks to the grid system. Apart from Lower Manhattan – where the thoroughfares twist, turn, and usually have names instead of numbers – all roads running from west to east are called 'streets' and those running from north to south are called 'avenues.' Streets are numbered from south to north and avenues from east to west. Some avenues also have names, such as York Avenue, Lexington Avenue, Park Avenue and Madison Avenue (street signs and addresses list Sixth Avenue as Avenue of the Americas, but New Yorkers rarely call it that). Inclusion of 'West' (W) or 'East' (E) in addresses shows whether it lies west or east of Fifth Avenue. There is just one avenue that doesn't conform to this pattern: Broadway cuts across the island diagonally.

DOWNTOWN

In Lower Manhattan, at the island's southern tip, is the oldest, most historic part of the city; the Financial District corresponds roughly to the area south of Worth Street, which begins just below Chinatown. Here you'll find Wall Street, One World Trade Center, the 9/11 Memorial, South Street Seaport, and ferries to Staten Island and the Statue of Liberty. After years of neglect, clubs and bars have moved in, making the area worth a visit even after 7pm. A good source of information on developments in Lower Manhattan is the Alliance for Downtown New York, Inc. at www.downtownny.com.

ONE WORLD TRADE CENTER AND 9/11 MEMORIAL

For decades, the most visible tourist attraction in Lower Manhattan was the World Trade Center. It was a huge complex of offices, a hotel, shopping malls, subway stations and the twin towers themselves. When the towers were opened in the 1970s, they were the tallest buildings in the world.

After September 11, 2001 – when the towers became the target of the country's worst terrorist attack – the construction site where

ICON OF HOPE

Remarkable as it might seem, a huge globe-shaped metal sculpture survived the tons of metal and concrete that crashed down upon it on 9/11. The *Sphere* by Fritz Koenig had stood for more than 30 years in the World Trade Center Plaza. In March 2002, it was moved to nearby Battery Park, where, on the first anniversary of the attack, an eternal flame was lit in memory of the victims. In 2017 the sculpture was returned to the World Trade Center where it will reside permanently in Liberty Park.

the complex once stood became a moving memorial. The former Ground Zero now holds as much, if not more meaning for visitors, as when they came to marvel at the buildings themselves. Today, the shimmering **One World Trade Center ❶** (formerly known as Freedom Tower) rises up at the center of the site, and the surrounding **9/11 Memorial** offers a tranquil place to reflect and honor the victims.

Completed in 2014 to a design by David M. Childs, One World Trade Center is the highest building in the Western Hemisphere, standing 1,776ft (541 meter) high. Its observation deck (www. oneworldobservatory.com; daily 10am–7pm, with exceptions) on the 102nd floor offers unrivalled views over the city. Access is provided thanks to a $4 billion transportation hub connecting subway, train, ferry, and bus lines in a striking structure designed by acclaimed Spanish architect Santiago Calatrava. Also connected to the transportation hub is the Cortlandt Street subway station which, after suffering severe damage in the September 11, 2001 terrorist attack, reopened in 2018.

The memorial, which incorporates the footprints of the twin towers into its design, was dedicated on the 10th anniversary of the attack. Visitors to the accompanying 9/11 Memorial Museum need to reserve a ticket from www.911memorial.org.

BATTERY PARK CITY

When the World Trade Center was being built in the late 1960s, some 30 million tons of excavated landfill were dumped on adjoining Hudson River docks to create the site of what became, in the 1980s, **Battery Park City**, a collection of high- and low-rise apartment and office buildings and parks. A lovely esplanade lined with parks and gardens stretches along the river from Stuyvesant High School on the north end, all the way south to historic Battery Park. The highlight of the adjacent **Brookfield Place** is the fine **Winter**

One World Trade Center

Garden, a public atrium ringed by shops, restaurants, and bars. Grab takeout from a café and join the traders on one of the benches, or enjoy a more upscale lunch at one of the sit-down restaurants.

A stroll down the promenade is a pleasant way to spend an hour, and also a great place to view the sunset. At the end of the promenade, near Bowling Green subway station, is the **Museum of Jewish Heritage** ❷ (www.mjhnyc.org; Sun–Tue 10am–6pm, Wed–Thu 10am–8pm, Fri 10am–5pm, until 3pm on Fri early Nov–mid-Mar, closed Sat and Jewish holidays). Beyond the first floor's interesting multimedia introductory show are galleries about Jewish life and culture; the second floor is devoted to the Holocaust, while the third floor contains exhibits about Judaism today. By focusing on the complexity of Jewish life in the 20th century, the museum gives a less harrowing account than others devoted solely to the Holocaust.

Nearby is **Battery Park**, a leafy expanse at the tip of Manhattan. Most visitors head for **Castle Clinton**. Originally the West Battery – a fortification to help protect ships in New York from the English navy – the building dates to 1811. By 1824 its military mission was fulfilled and the fort became a concert hall, immigration checkpoint, and even for a while, the New York City Aquarium. The National Park Service took over the building in the 1940s and renamed it Castle Clinton. It was re-opened in 1975 as a small museum and as the ticket office for ferries to the Statue of Liberty and Ellis Island (see page 27).

Across from Battery Park's northern tip, at the foot of Broadway, is a small triangular patch called **Bowling Green**. It is said that this is where in 1626, Peter Minuit bought Manhattan from Native Americans for the equivalent of $24. Today it is the site of one of New York's many Greenmarkets, selling fresh local produce (Tue and Thu 8am–5pm).

Looming over the square is the **Old Customs House**, which is now the home of the **National Museum of the American Indian** ❸ (www.americanindian.si.edu; Mon–Fri 10am–5pm), a branch of the Smithsonian Institution in Washington, DC. The museum celebrates Native American culture and showcases a variety of artifacts. The other Smithsonian branch in NYC is the Cooper Hewitt, Smithsonian Design Museum, on the Upper East Side.

STATUE OF LIBERTY AND ELLIS ISLAND

Ferries for the Statue of Liberty and Ellis Island leave from **Battery Park**, calling first at the Statue of Liberty (www.cityexperiences.com/new-york/city-cruises/statue; daily 8.30am–5pm in summer, until 3.30pm in winter; departures every 20 mins).

Castle Clinton

The **Statue of Liberty** ❹ is the most recognized icon of New York City. Some 10 years in the making, it was a gift from France in recognition of the friendship between the two countries and has served as a beacon for immigrants arriving in the New World for over 100 years. Frédéric-Auguste Bartholdi's 151ft (46m) tall creation is one of those wild dreams that became reality. Engineering expertise had to be harnessed to art, so Bartholdi called in Gustave Eiffel to work on the complex skeletal framework. Parisian workmen erected the statue in 1884, as bemused Parisians watched her crowned head rise above their rooftops. It was later dismantled and shipped in 214 huge wooden crates for re-assembly on Liberty Island. The statue of Liberty Enlightening the World was unveiled by President Cleveland on October 28, 1886.

There are several options for visiting the monument and all must be booked through Statue City Cruises (see above). A basic cruise ticket will get you to Liberty Island, with access to the Statue of Liberty Museum and grounds. To access the interior of the

LIBERTY SCIENCE CENTER

From the docks outside Brookfield Place, you can take the New York Waterway Ferry to Paulus Hook Ferry Terminal in New Jersey (www.nywaterway.com; every 7–8 minutes on weekdays) to connect to the Hudson-Bergen Light Rail (Essex Street Station to Liberty State Park Station; www.njtransit.com) for the **Liberty Science Center** (www.lsc.org; daily 9am–5.30pm). Though not technically a New York City attraction, it is nevertheless a fun place to explore. The exhibitions are designed to appeal to all ages and include a skyscraper area, where visitors can walk along a beam above the exhibition floor and see beams recovered from the World Trade Center. The center also includes an IMAX theater.

statue itself, you must buy a pedestal ticket, which grants access to the base. A few hundred daily crown tickets are also usually available for those who plan ahead and are able to climb the steep steps to the top of the crown. Please note that many restrictions apply to crown tickets, including minimum height requirements, and that access was suspended indefinitely during the Covid-19 pandemic.

Once you arrive on Liberty Island you can learn about the history of the statue with free tours led by Park Rangers. Inside the museum visitors can view the original torch then proceed to the promenade area for an up-close view of the statue and a spectacular view of New York Harbor. It is a strenuous climb up the 377 narrow steps to the crown but if you're lucky enough to snag a ticket, you'll be rewarded with a great view. The torch remains closed to the public as it has been since 1916.

After the statue, the ferry continues to **Ellis Island 5**. The island itself was mostly created from landfill from the building of the New York subway system. The museum, which opened in 1990, retraces, through film, audio-visual displays, and exhibitions, the sufferings and joys of some 12 million immigrants who entered the United States through these doors between 1892 and 1954, when overseas consulates took over the screening process. You

Staten Island Ferry

If you are on a tight budget, a ride on the free Staten Island Ferry is a great way to get a closer look at the Statue of Liberty. There is little of interest to visitors on Staten Island, but the 20-minute ferry ride is well worth the trip. Catch the ferry from the southern tip of Battery Park and you'll get stunning views of the Statue of Liberty and the Manhattan skyline, and since the ferry runs 24 hours a day, you can get the same view at night.

The Statue of Liberty

might find a long-lost family member on the Immigrant Wall of Honor. Among notable personalities who made it through Ellis Island were actors Charlie Chaplin, Claudette Colbert, Bob Hope, composer Irving Berlin, the Von Trapp family of *The Sound of Music* fame, and author Rudyard Kipling.

FRAUNCES TAVERN

Near the ferry terminal, at 54 Pearl Street (at Broad Street) is **Fraunces Tavern**. First opened for business in 1762, this is where George Washington is said to have bid farewell to his officers after the Revolutionary War. The building you see today is mostly a recreation, built in 1907. Colonial history buffs may appreciate the modest museum upstairs (www.frauncestavernmuseum.org; Wed–Sun noon–5pm): exhibits include documents and period furniture, as well as items such as a lock of Washington's hair, a fragment of one of his teeth, and a shoe that belonged to his wife, Martha. Others may opt to dine in the pseudo-colonial atmosphere of the restaurant downstairs, together with bankers and brokers (www.frauncestavern.com; daily noon–2am).

The immediate area is absolutely teeming with remnants of old New York. After leaving Fraunces Tavern, if you walk to the right on Pearl Street and turn left at the next corner, you'll come to **Stone Street**, another historic district with a colonial street plan and buildings that were formerly dry goods warehouses and stores.

At the other end of Stone Street, after a quick jog to the right, you will be back on Pearl Street and Hanover Square, which was a wealthy neighborhood during colonial days. Two blocks south of the tavern, at the end of Broad Street, you will find the southern tip of the island and the terminal for the ferries to Staten Island and Governor's Island (www.govisland.com; daily May–Oct).

WALL STREET

If you continue on Pearl Street, after a couple of blocks you will come to **Wall Street ❻**, perhaps one of the most famous streets in the world, if only for its metaphoric heft. There was once an actual wall here, built in 1653 by Dutch governor Peter Stuyvesant to protect New Amsterdam from the encroaching British. Turn left on Wall Street to find several buildings of note. Number 55 Wall Street, which dates to 1842, is one of the oldest buildings on the street. The tallest, at 927ft (283m), is 40 Wall Street. Now known as the **Trump Building**, this was briefly the world's tallest structure, before it was eclipsed by the Chrysler Building's spire. The skyscrapers here are closer together than at any other place in the city, leading locals to dub them the 'canyons' of Lower Manhattan.

At 26 Wall Street (at Nassau), you will see a large statue of Washington

Fraunces Tavern

The Brooklyn Bridge and Lower Manhattan skyline

outside **Federal Hall National Memorial** (www.nps.gov/feha; check website for current hours), which was formerly the US Customs building. The original building, demolished in 1812, was the home of the US government for a year when New York was briefly the nation's capital (1785–90); it was also where Washington took the oath as the first president of the US, on April 30, 1789.

Most visitors to the city are more interested in the building across the street, the **New York Stock Exchange**, at 8–18 Broad Street. Interestingly, though Wall Street is synonymous with stock trading, the building's entrance is on the cross street. The NYSE is no longer open to the public for visits or tours.

BROOKLYN BRIDGE

There are a few other sights of interest to visitors in Lower Manhattan. At the corner of Broadway and Fulton streets is **St Paul's Chapel** and its churchyard. George Washington worshiped here after his inauguration; you can see the pew in which he sat, to your right as you enter.

A little farther up at 233 Broadway stands the **Woolworth Building**, which reigned as the world's tallest building from 1913 until the Chrysler Building ushered in the skyscraper age in 1930. You can't go upstairs, but tours take in the ornate lobby and mezzanine level (www.woolworthtours.com). Just up Broadway is **New York City Hall**, which is fairly unassuming. And if you are in the mood for a stroll, there is none more scenic or interesting than a trip by foot across the **Brooklyn Bridge 7**, which opened in 1883. Before it was built, the only way across to Brooklyn was by ferry. The entrance to the pedestrian walkway is on the east side of City Hall Park; take a walk all the way to Brooklyn Heights.

One more detour may be in order for history buffs. At the intersection of Fulton and Water streets, the 60-foot-tall (18-meter) **Titanic Memorial Lighthouse** was erected in 1913 in memory of those lost on the ill-fated ocean liner.

SOUTH STREET SEAPORT

A final area of interest in this part of Lower Manhattan is the **South Street Seaport**. At the foot of Fulton Street on the East River, this 11-acre (4-hectare), nine-block enclave was once in the middle of the nation's busiest working docks. Yet its usefulness faded, and the area was turned into a pedestrian mall in the 1960s. The **South Street Seaport Museum**, (www.southstreetseaportmuseum.org; Wed–Sun 11am–7pm) at 12 Fulton Street, offers a glimpse into the nautical heritage of the city.

Occupying **Pier 17 8** is a glass fronted multi-use building overlooking the East River. Retail space houses top brands and restaurants as well as a Market Hall which offers healthy fast foods and produce. The roof top is open for concerts, cinema screenings and sports classes as well as hosting pop-up bars in the summer.

WEST MIDTOWN – THEATER DISTRICT

When visitors think of New York and the Big Apple, this intersection of Broadway and Seventh Avenue is usually considered the center of it all. It is also the heart of the Broadway theater district.

TIMES SQUARE AND BROADWAY

Once a seedy, unpleasant place, **Times Square ❾** lies at the intersection of Broadway and Seventh Avenue, at the heart of Manhattan's theater district. This is roughly the area between 42nd and 53rd streets, between Sixth and Eighth avenues. Back in the *Taxi Driver* years of the 1970s, it had reached a distinct low point. For a time, the area may have been the 'crossroads of the world,' but perhaps only for the down and out.

All that changed in the mid-1990s in Mayor Rudolf Giuliani's clean-up of the area. Long gone are the hustlers, pornographic theaters and bookstores; in their place are smart office buildings, hotels, stores, restaurants, and other attractions that appeal to New Yorkers and tourists. Even the traffic jams are gone. Broadway from 47th to

BROADWAY

The name Broadway is synonymous with glitz, glamour, theaters, shows, musicals and entertainment. The Great White Way, referring to the stretch between 40th and 53rd streets, takes its pseudonym from when it was first lit with electric lighting. Its heyday was in the 1920s and '30s, when there were over 80 theaters on and around Broadway. The most famous section was 42nd Street, so famous in fact that theater owners with properties on 41st or 43rd Street, built passageways through entire blocks just to be able to boast a 'Forty-Second Street' address.

Times Square

42nd streets is now entirely pedestrianized. One can debate whether this change has made the area blander, but it certainly has been revived. The 'square' is named for the *New York Times*, whose headquarters was once at 1 Times Square, where the ball still drops on New Year's Eve. The *Times* has since moved premises twice, most recently to a 52-story skyscraper on 40th Street, but the square's name will probably never change. Other features of the square include the cylindrical NASDAQ Building at 43rd and Broadway, its huge electronic display providing up-to-the-minute financial news. At the corner of 44th Street is the Viacom building, where MTV's Times Square Studio is located. On the east side of the Square (also at 44th Street), is the corner studio for *Good Morning America*.

NORTH OF TIMES SQUARE

Across Broadway (between Seventh Avenue and Broadway at 47th Street), you can't miss the glowing red steps in **Father Duffy**

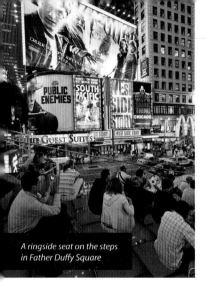

A ringside seat on the steps in Father Duffy Square

Square, the northern triangle of Times Square. Enjoy a break on the steps as you watch the hustle and bustle of the Times Square. Under the steps you will find the TKTS booth, which offers discounted tickets for same-day Broadway and off-Broadway plays and musicals.

Further north at 1697 Broadway is the Ed Sullivan Theater, where *The Late Show with Stephen Colbert* is based. At 131 W. 55th Street (between Sixth and Seventh avenues) is New York **City Center** (www.nycitycenter.org), a former Shriners temple that now serves as an ornate Moorish-style theater. Two blocks north is **Carnegie Hall** (154 W. 57th Street; www.carnegiehall.org), one of New York's most famous performing arts spaces; the main concert hall (the Isaac Stern Auditorium) is said to have the best acoustics in New York.

WEST 42ND STREET

West of Times Square, on 42nd Street are some of the refurbished theaters and entertainment centers. On the north side of 42nd Street is the **New Victory Theater**, which specializes in children's productions; further along 42nd are two movie theaters facing each other across the street, the 13-screen Regal **E-Walk** entertainment complex and the 25-screen **AMC Empire**. On the south side of 42nd Street is a **Madame Tussaud's Wax Museum**. On the northeast corner of 42nd and Broadway is 4 Times Square, formerly the **Condé Nast Building**.

At Eighth Avenue, is the **Port Authority of New York**, the city's main bus station. Once the scariest place in Manhattan, it is still not picturesque, but is a thriving and not unpleasant commuter hub. Today the neighborhood is dominated by the **New York Times Building**, completed in 2007; it ties with the Chrysler Building (see page 45) as the 12th-tallest building in New York.

At the far western end of 42nd Street, Pier 83 is the home to the **Circle Line**, which offers cruises around Manhattan (see page 96). A little further north, on Pier 86, at 46th Street and Twelfth Avenue, is the popular **Intrepid Sea, Air & Space Museum⓾** (www.intrepidmuseum.org; daily 10am–5pm, until 6pm on summer weekends). The Intrepid, a decommissioned US Navy aircraft carrier, is packed with exhibits on sea exploration and warfare, space travel, and aviation. You will also find here the submarine USS *Growler*, a Concorde supersonic airliner, and the space shuttle *Enterprise*.

CENTRAL MIDTOWN

Midtown has a wealth of cultural and shopping attractions, from art (MoMA), to literature (New York Public Library) and the department stores of Fifth Avenue.

BRYANT PARK

East of Times Square on 42nd Street, between Sixth and Fifth avenues, are the green and leafy expanses of **Bryant Park**, another great New York restoration project of the early 1990s. The present French-style layout of the park dates from the Great

Carnegie Hall

Financed by the iron and steel magnate Andrew Carnegie, Carnegie Hall was first opened in 1891. It is one of the great music venues of the city. If you can't make it to a concert here, at least have a look at the excellent museum.

Depression, but by the 1980s it had become a no man's land of drug dealers night and day. Now it is one of midtown's most pleasant oases, where office workers gather in the summer months for lunch or just to relax. Next to the park is the **New York Public Library** ⓫ (www.nypl.org), a grand Beaux-Arts-style building that dates to 1911; two handsome, famous and much-photographed stone lions, Patience and Fortitude, flag its Fifth Avenue entrance. One of the largest research libraries in the world, the structure houses several million books, almost as many manuscripts, and several vast reading rooms. The main reading room has been modernized, but nevertheless retains its original grandeur. Changing exhibitions are regularly mounted in the library's exhibition halls.

ROCKEFELLER CENTER

The centerpiece of central Manhattan, covering 22 acres (9 hectares) between Fifth and Sixth avenues, from 47th to 51st streets, is **Rockefeller Center** ⓬. The buildings in this complex are linked by underground walkways and concourses, which are themselves filled with shops, a post office, and restaurants. Columbia University purchased the site in 1811 when it was still farmland. In 1928, John D. Rockefeller, a founder of the Standard Oil Company, asked the university for a lease on the site to raise a commercial complex. Built

Diamond District

West 47th is New York's Diamond District, an area dominated by mostly Orthodox Jewish diamond dealers; unbelievably, the majority of the diamonds that pass through New York find their way to this unassuming street. While this may be a good place to shop for diamonds, it is questionable as to whether or not you'll find any real bargains at the jewelry or 'discount' electronics stores.

New York Public Library

mostly between 1931 and 1940, Rockefeller Center attracts thousands of office-workers, visitors, and shoppers daily.

From Fifth Avenue you enter via the **Channel Gardens**, a sloping walkway divided by fountains and flowerbeds between the British and French buildings, which end at the sunken plaza and its famous ice rink (in winter) and gilded **statue of Prometheus**. This is also where the giant Christmas tree is placed (right behind Prometheus). If you have time, wander around and admire some of the Art Deco details.

Nowadays, the former GE Building, now **30 Rockefeller Center** or Comcast Building (30 Rockefeller Plaza, the largest building in the complex) is better known as the headquarters for the NBC television network and the *Today Show*; the glassed-in studio is across the street from the building's southeast corner, at 49th Street.

The Comcast's observation deck is called **Top of the Rock** (entrance on W. 50th Street; www.topoftherocknyc.com; daily

Statue of Prometheus

10am–10pm), and offers visitors an unparalleled and unobstructed 360degree view of the city from the 70th floor. The elevator to the top features a transparent ceiling so that visitors can view their rapid ascent all the way up the elevator chute. A light show and projected images add to the fun of the ride.

Also at this corner is the **The Shop at NBC Studios**, a combination attraction and merchandise store festooned with the logos of the network and some of its television shows. You can also purchase tickets here for the extremely popular NBC Studio Tour (www.thetouratnbcstudios.com; suspended during Covid-19 pandemic, see website for updates).

Radio City Music Hall (corner of Sixth Avenue and 50th Street) is one of the largest theaters in the world, with a seating capacity of around 6,000. This restored Art Deco masterpiece is a popular location for seasonal theme shows, including the dazzling Christmas Spectacular; it's also the home of the ever-popular Rockettes. Tours can be arranged by tel: 866-858-0007, or at www.msg.com/radio-city-music-hall.

FIFTH AVENUE

At the turn of the 20th century, **Fifth Avenue** was the location of some of the largest and most opulent mansions in New York. After World War I, a number of fashionable and expensive stores opened for business here. You'll still find Saks Fifth Avenue (50th Street), Cartier (52nd Street), Tiffany's (57th Street), and Bergdorf Goodman (58th Street), though most of the trendiest designers now have their boutiques on Madison Avenue or in SoHo. The gaudiest building on Fifth Avenue is without a doubt Donald Trump's 1980s **Trump Tower** (56th and 57th streets), where a 'wall' of water slides down rose marble set between gleaming brass escalator rails.

St Patrick's Cathedral ⓭, on Fifth Avenue (50th and 51st), was the tallest building in the vicinity when it was built between 1858 and 1879. Today, it appears somewhat dwarfed by the skyscrapers of Rockefeller Center and the apartment building next door, though the juxtaposition of its soft gray granite and the surrounding glass creates a stunning image. Seat of the Archdiocese of New York City, the church is the focal point of the Irish parade on St Patrick's Day.

At the corner of Fifth Avenue and 59th Street, busy **Grand Army Plaza** marks the division between Fifth Avenue's shopping area and the residential section, which is lined with exclusive apartment buildings and a few remaining mansions. This is the place to hire a horse-drawn carriage for a ride round Central Park (see page 55). It is also the site of two of New York's most famous hotels, the **Plaza** and the **Pierre** (at East 61st Street).

Top of the Rock, Rockefeller Center

St Patrick's Cathedral

Across from the plaza is the General Motors Building. A distinctive 32ft (10m) glass cube in front of it marks the entrance to the subterranean **Apple Store** (767 Fifth Avenue), where you can browse the latest cutting-edge iPads, iPhones, and other Apple products 365 days a year, 24 hours a day.

MUSEUM OF MODERN ART

One of midtown's most important cultural centers is the **Museum of Modern Art** ⑭, or MoMA (www.moma.org; Sun–Fri 10.30am–5.30pm, Sat 10.30am–7pm), located on 53rd Street between Fifth and Sixth avenues. From 2002–2004, a complete redesign by architect Yoshio Taniguchi doubled the museum's exhibition space and another major renovation, completed in 2019, transformed the museum entirely. The main change is that work will rotate every six to nine months – with a handful of exceptions, even MoMA's most popular paintings will now move around. If there's a special work you want to see, check the website in advance, which has up-to-date information about where each piece is currently located. Each floor is still divided chiefly by chronology, but the other major innovation is that individual galleries are now thematically based and mix mediums – photography, drawings, video, and sculpture presented alongside traditional paintings

Devoted to works of art created after 1880, roughly from the Impressionists on, the collection includes such masterpieces as Dalí's *The Persistence of Memory*, Van Gogh's *The Starry Night*, Rousseau's *Sleeping Gypsy*, Wyeth's *Christina's World* and Warhol's *Gold Marilyn Monroe*. The collection also includes a number of Monet's Water Lilies, as well as important works by Picasso, Jackson Pollock, Mark Rothko and Chuck Close.

Modern sculpture and design is not ignored, and there are examples of everything from Marcel Duchamp's Bicycle Wheel to huge installations by contemporary artists. The modern sculpture garden remains a distinctive element of MoMA.

The flagship MoMA design store, a great place to buy artistically designed household wares, is located within the museum; a second store is across the street at 44 West 53rd Street. There is a third in SoHo (81 Spring Street).

EAST MIDTOWN

In this area you will spend much of your time looking up at major architectural landmarks, including the ceiling of Grand Central and the Chrysler Building.

MADISON AND PARK AVENUES

The streets east of Fifth Avenue have several places of interest to visitors. The 57-story tower of the **Lotte New York Palace Hotel** (East 50th and 51st) incorporates the historic Villard Houses,

Museum of Modern Art (MoMA)

Grand Central Terminal

which date to 1882. Take a walk through the grand lobby if you are in the area.

A Park Avenue landmark is the **Waldorf-Astoria Hotel**, which takes up the entire block between Park and Lexington from 49th to 50th. It has been host to world leaders since 1931. Nearby, the bronze-and-glass **Seagram Building**, on Park Avenue between 52nd and 53rd, is the only New York building designed by Mies van der Rohe. Across the street, at 390 Park Avenue, is the 24-story **Lever House**. Built in 1952 it was one of the first glass-walled office buildings in the States.

GRAND CENTRAL AND THE CHRYSLER BUILDING

A complete restoration and renovation project in the late 1990s returned **Grand Central Terminal** ⓯ (at 42nd between Park and Lexington) to its former splendor. Completed in 1913, the building is a Beaux-Arts masterpiece. Inside, more than 40 platforms split between two levels serve dozens of rail lines. The central concourse is vast but also light, airy, and harmonious under a blue-green, star-sprinkled ceiling 12 stories tall. It is invaded every afternoon from 4–6pm by hundreds of thousands of suburban commuters catching their trains home to points north of Manhattan. If you enter from the Vanderbilt Avenue side, look across the lobby to see the grand staircase. Inside the station are restaurants, shops, and, on the lower level, the famous **Oyster Bar & Restaurant**, a favorite for power-lunchers.

Across Lexington Avenue on 42nd Street stands the most beautiful skyscraper of all, the **Chrysler Building** ⑯, a silvery Art-Deco needle completed in 1930. For a few months it was the tallest structure in the world, but it was rapidly surpassed by the Empire State Building (see page 46). The stylized eagle heads on the upper corners were modeled on the Chrysler automobile's 1929 radiator cap.

At the corner of Second Avenue, even more fine Art Deco architecture distinguishes the former **Daily News Building**; the lobby, with its huge revolving globe, is well worth a look. The paper moved to a new location west of Penn Station in the mid-1990s. Also well worth a look is the **Ford Foundation** headquarters (320 East 43rd Street); offices open onto a spacious interior court with trees – New York's first office building atrium. It's another of the city's fine public spaces.

UNITED NATIONS

The eastern end of 42nd Street used to be a warren of tenements and slaughterhouses, but thanks to John D.

Touring Grand Central

75-minute tours of Grand Central Station are offered daily at 12.30pm by the Municipal Arts Society of New York (the tour begins in front of the entrance to Track 29 in the Main Concourse; tel: 212-935 3960; www.nyc.docentour. com). The tour covers the publicly accessible areas of the terminal, including the building's exterior and its context within the neighborhood. Each tour differs slightly but should include the Main Concourse, the Lower Concourse, Vanderbilt Hall, the Campbell Apartment, the Whispering Gallery and Terminal City. Alternatively, download an app for iPhone and Android phones at www. orpheogroup.com/us/the-official-grand-central-tour-app for a self-guided tour.

Rockefeller, Jr., it is now the home of the **United Nations** 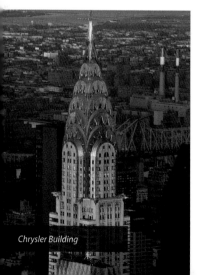. A team of architects, including Wallace K. Harrison, Le Corbusier, and Oscar Niemeyer, designed the buildings. They were completed in the early 1950s. The Secretariat is housed in the glass-and-marble structure, while the General Assembly meets in the lower building with the slightly concave roof. The flags of the member nations flutter from the flagpoles along First Avenue.

When the General Assembly is not in session, visitors from around the world can usually take daily multilingual tours (http://visit.un.org; guided tours suspended due to Covid-19, check website for the latest information) of the General Assembly Hall and Council Chambers, the sculptures in the grounds overlooking the East River and Queens, and informative documentary exhibits. A highlight is the meditation room adorned with stained-glass windows by Chagall.

SOUTH MIDTOWN

EMPIRE STATE BUILDING

The **Empire State Building** 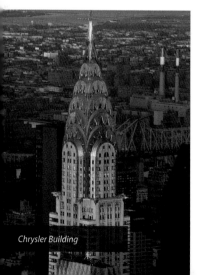 (corner of Fifth Avenue and 34th Street; www.esb-nyc.com; daily noon–9pm, with exceptions) no longer holds the title of tallest building in the world. Yet, it is otherwise everything a skyscraper should be: 102 stories; 60,000 tons of steel; 3,500 miles (5,632km) of

Chrysler Building

telephone wires and cables; 60 miles (97km) of pipes; a total volume of 1.25 million cubic yards (1 million cubic meters); 1,860 steps, and of course, its towering height – 1,453ft (443m), including the lightning rod (overall, half as tall again as the Eiffel Tower). It is a well-worn cultural icon, appearing in movies from *King Kong* and *An Affair to Remember* to *Sleepless in Seattle*. Opened in 1931 in the depths of the Great Depression, the build-

The Empire State Building

ing took just two years to complete. The 86th-floor Observation Deck provides stunning views of New York. On the outside terrace you can see much of Manhattan, including Central Park, and on a clear day you can see ships 40 miles (64km) away. You can also visit the 102nd floor observatory (extra charge).

Back on earth, you can walk west along 34th Street to visit **Macy's** (Sixth and Seventh avenues), New York's most famous and largest department store. Nearby, at Seventh Avenue and 33rd Street, is **Madison Square Garden**, renowned for boxing matches and rock concerts. In addition to being home to the New York Knicks (basketball) and the Rangers (ice hockey), it is also used as a conference center. The Garden seats 20,000 people and its adjacent theater can take an additional 5,000. Under Madison Square Garden is Pennsylvania Station (usually referred to as Penn Station), the railway terminal for New Jersey and Long Island com-muters and the Manhattan stop for Amtrak. Across Eighth Avenue

Taking in the view from the Empire State's observation deck

is the **General Post Office**, which was a twin to the old Penn Station, torn down in the late 1960s to make room for Madison Square Garden. Most of the old post office has now been transformed into Moynihan Station, an expansion of Penn Station under Eighth Avenue, opened in 2020, along with a new rail tunnel below the Hudson River which connects to Penn Station.

If you are in town for a trade show, chances are that you will head for the **Jacob K. Javits Convention Center** (www.javitscenter.com), the city's largest exhibition center, a striking building on Eleventh Avenue between 34th and 37th streets. Designed by I. M. Pei, the center was named for New York state's long-time Republican senator.

To the east of the Empire State Building, at 36th and Madison in Murray Hill, is another prominent landmark: the **Morgan Library & Museum** (www.themorgan.org). The personal collection of J. Pierpont Morgan includes rare books and manuscripts, three

Gutenberg Bibles and Florentine sculpture and art. Often overlooked by tourists, it is a quiet place, which is one of its pleasures.

UPPER EAST SIDE – THE MUSEUM MILE

Home to many famous museums, the Upper East Side starts at 59th Street, at the corner of Central Park. Beyond the east 60s, much of this area is residential, and includes some of Manhattan's most expensive real estate.

Most of the Upper East Side's museums are located along the 'Museum Mile' from 82nd to 110th streets. But there are a few exceptions. One is the **Mount Vernon Hotel Museum and Garden**, at 421 East 61st Street (First and York avenues; www. mvhm.org; Tue–Sun 11am–4pm). This Federal-style house, which dates from 1799, is an interesting period piece for those with time and interest, featuring 19th-century furnishings and decorative arts.

CITYPASS

One way to see several of Manhattan's top attractions and to save some money at the same time is to buy a CityPass. The pass gives you admission to six leading attractions for only $136, considerably less than the total for individual full admission prices. Attractions include the Empire State Building Observation Deck, the Metropolitan Museum of Art, the American Museum of Natural History, the Guggenheim Museum or Top of the Rock, Circle Line Sightseeing Cruises or Statue of Liberty and Ellis Island and 9/11 Museum or the Intrepid Sea, Air & Space Museum. The pass can be used for nine consecutive days and should enable you to avoid most ticket lines. Buy it online at www.citypass.com, or at any of the participating attractions.

FRICK MADISON

A few other major museums are just off the Museum Mile proper. The **Frick Madison** ⑲ at 945 Madison Avenue (www.frick.org; see website for current hours), containing the remarkable art collection of steel magnate Henry Clay Frick (1849–1919), will be displayed in the Breuer Building until at least the end of 2023, when a massive renovation of the Frick Mansion (1 East 70th St) should be complete. Henry Frick put together one of the finest private collections of art in the US, and upon the death of Frick's widow in 1931, their home, and the art therein, were donated to the city of New York. The Breuer Building was the former premises of the Whitney Museum of American Art. Designed by architect Marcel Breuer, the building's Brutalist style caused much controversy when it debuted in 1966. Most of the Frick collection has been

The Garden Court, The Frick Collection

temporarily exhibited inside. In addition to three Vermeers (including Mistress and Maid), the museum holds fine works by Hans Holbein (Sir Thomas More and Thomas Cromwell), El Greco (St. Jerome), Bellini (St. Francis in Ecstasy), Boucher, Titian, Goya, Whistler, Rembrandt, and Velázquez; exquisite European furniture; and one of the largest collections of small bronze sculptures in the world.

Asia Society

The attractive redgranite building on the northeast corner of Park Avenue and 70th Street is the headquarters of the Asia Society (www.asiasociety. org; Wed–Sun 11am–5pm, with exceptions). The society mounts regular, imaginative exhibitions of ancient and modern Asian and Pacific art, assembled from private collections, as well as from its own permanent collection.

METROPOLITAN MUSEUM OF ART

Museum Mile begins at the **Metropolitan Museum of Art** ⓴, located at 82nd Street and Fifth Avenue (www.metmuseum.org; Sun–Tue and Thu 10am–5pm, Fri–Sat 10am–9pm). Monumentally huge, the 'Met,' as it is affectionately known, is a repository for all things cultural, from Egyptian mummies to Roman bronzes, Chinese pottery and wonderful Impressionist paintings. Founded in 1870, the institution owns over 2 million items, though only around a quarter of the total collection is on display at any one time in its nearly 250 rooms. The Art of the Arab Lands galleries are worth a closer look, especially the textiles and the stunning 16th-century decorative ceiling of interlocking stars and polygons. More than 5,300 works of classical art are on show in the refurbished Greek and Roman galleries. Children love the Egyptian treasures, especially the Temple of Dendur, which sits in its own room. There's also audio guides designed especially for kids.

Don't miss the American Wing, particularly the Garden Court, where stained-glass windows, fountains, sculptures, plants and benches create a tranquil environment. On all sides are period rooms and other galleries that show off the Met's fine holdings in American art. Among the famous paintings are Emanuel Leutze's *Washington Crossing the Delaware*, Albert Bierstadt's *The Rocky Mountains*, as well as notable works by Winslow Homer.

European paintings, sculpture, and decorative arts before 1800 include Botticelli's *Last Communion of St. Jerome*, Giovanni di Paolo's *Adoration of the Magi*, Rembrandt's *Self-Portrait, 1660*, and works by Bellini, Ingres, El Greco, Holbein, Goya, and virtually any other famous painter you can name. Similarly stellar is the collection of 19th-century European paintings and sculptures, including works by such luminaries as Van Gogh, Monet, Renoir, and Degas. The Robert Lehman Collection, at the west end of the main floor, comprises fine Old Masters and Italian Renaissance paintings, including several period rooms recreated from Lehman's home. The Michael C. Rockefeller Wing houses a good collection of primitive art.

The Lila Acheson Wallace Wing, devoted to modern art, remains one of the most popular sections of the Met. It features paintings, sculptures, and decorative arts from Europe and America,

Portrait of Adele Bloch-Bauer I by Gustav Klimt in the Neue Galerie

including Picasso's *Gertrude Stein* and works by major modern artists including Jackson Pollock, Willem de Kooning, Edward Hopper, Georgia O'Keefe, Diego Rivera, Frank Stella, and Chuck Close. Modern sculpture is often on view in the roof garden overlooking Central Park, where there is a café in the summer. On top of all this, the Met has one of the best art bookstores in the US.

NEUE GALERIE

Four blocks north of the Met (1048 Fifth Avenue at 86th Street) is the **Neue Galerie** (www.neuegalerie.com; Thu–Mon 11am–5pm), a small but unique museum that specializes in early 20th-century German and Austrian art and design, featuring works by Gustav Klimt and various Bauhaus exponents. Its increased popularity is largely thanks to the 2015 film Woman in Gold, starring Helen Mirren, which told the remarkable story of the museum's star painting, Gustav Klimt's Portrait of Adele Bloch-Bauer I, a resplendent example of Klimt's "Golden Period", stolen by the Nazis. The museum is housed in an elegant mansion built in 1914 for the industrialist William Starr Miller by Carrère and Hastings, architects of the New York Public Library; the building was once occupied by society doyenne, Mrs Cornelius Vanderbilt III. The Café Sabarsky inside (see page 113) is a recommended stop too.

GUGGENHEIM MUSEUM

At 89th Street is the **Solomon R. Guggenheim Museum** ❹ (www. guggenheim.org; Sun–Mon and Wed–Fri 11am–6pm, Sat 11am–8pm, with exceptions). The building, which was designed by Frank Lloyd Wright and opened in 1959, is now a New York landmark. The museum's most famous feature is perhaps not its paintings but the continuous spiral ramp that connects the building's six storeys.

The permanent collection, built on Guggenheim's original private collection of contemporary paintings, includes works by such artists as Brancusi, Klee, Chagall, Picasso, Miró, Calder, and Kandinsky. The Justin K. Thannhauser collection, in the annex, contains paintings by Renoir, Monet, Cézanne, Van Gogh, Gauguin, and Degas. The museum's collection is actually now spread somewhat thinly among its various branches in such disparate places as Bilbao, Las Vegas, Venice, and Berlin.

OTHER MUSEUMS

Nearby, at 91st Street, is the **Cooper-Hewitt, Smithsonian Design Museum** (www.cooperhewitt.org; Thu–Mon 10am–6pm). Housed in an elegant mansion completed for industrialist Andrew Carnegie in 1902, the Cooper-Hewitt is a slick, contemporary museum, with vast holdings of furniture, wall-coverings, textiles, prints, drawings, and miscellaneous objects.

MoMA

At 92nd Street, the **Jewish Museum** (www.thejewish-museum.org; Mon and Thu 11am–6pm, Fri 11am–4pm, Sat and Sun 10am–6pm), housed in the gothic Felix Warburg Mansion, is an important cultural and historical museum. It holds an extensive collection of Judaica and exhibits the work of Jewish artists.

Special exhibitions

Visitors should look out for special exhibitions at the Met; your standard entry will cover admission and no additional ticket is required to see them.

The **Museum of the City of New York** (www.mcny.org; daily 10am–6pm) is located at 103rd Street. This treasury of materials documenting New York City's history also includes a superb toy collection. The last institution on Museum Mile is **El Museo del Barrio** (www.elmuseo.org; Tue–Sat 11am–6pm, Sun noon–5pm), at 104th Street. Americans of Hispanic origin live in many parts of the city's boroughs, but El Barrio – the Quarter – in East (or Spanish) Harlem was the first predominantly Puerto Rican district. The museum is devoted to Latin American culture and art.

The long-gestating **Africa Center** (www.theafricacenter.org), a successor of the former Museum for African Art, at 110th Street has extended the Museum Mile to the northeastern tip of Central Park. Check their website for opening details.

CENTRAL PARK

The heart (some say the lungs) of Manhattan is **Central Park**, located between 59th and 110th streets and Fifth and Eighth avenues. This vast green space is half a mile wide and 2.5 miles long (0.8km x 4km) and is one of the main places where New Yorkers go to play. On summer weekends, residents (and visitors) come

The Guggenheim

by the thousands to play ball, skate, stroll, picnic, or listen to music. But the park is busy all week and all year long. The park's designers were Frederick Law Olmsted and Calvert Vaux, and the project, which began in 1858, took almost 20 years to complete. Creating a usable public space from a huge, sparse, and rocky landscape was a remarkable achievement for the time and revolutionized landscape architecture. Amazingly, almost everything you see in the park today, from the Great Lawn to the lakes, to the meadows and forest in the northern end, was constructed. The park is now partially supported, administered, and overseen by the Central Park Conservancy (www.centralparknyc.org).

There is always something going on in the park, from a concert to a rally to a bicycle race. To learn more about the park you can take a walking tour. The Central Park Conservancy sponsors free guided tours year-round, rain or shine, and downloadable audio tours (see the schedule and find downloads at www.centralparknyc.org). The more active will be interested in ball fields, tennis courts, boating, bouldering and horseback riding. Since most of the park's roads are closed on weekends, strolling, biking, and rollerskating are popular. Ice skating in Central Park is also a popular choice with rinks open from late October to early April, weather permitting.

PARK HIGHLIGHTS

Highlights in the southern end of the park include **Wollman Rink** (mid-Park at 63rd Street; www.wollmanrinknyc.com), which is used for ice-skating in the winter (Nov–Mar). A children's amusement park takes over during the summer months. There's another skating rink in the northern end of the park (between W. 106th and 108th streets); previously known as Lasker Rink, it will reopen as the Harlem Meer Center in 2024, with a swimming pool available in summer.

Closer to Fifth Avenue is the **Central Park Zoo ㉒**, including the **Tisch Children's Zoo** (www.centralparkzoo.com; Apr–Oct Mon–Fri 10am–5pm, Sat–Sun 10am–5.30pm, Nov–Mar daily 10am–4.30pm). In between is the Delacorte Musical Clock, which chimes the hours with musical animals. The highlights of the zoo include the sea-lion pool and polar bear house. Kids will love the petting zoo and the 'Enchanted Forest.' The admission charge for Central Park Zoo includes entrance to the children's zoo, and both are open daily.

Another favorite in the southeast corner of the park is the historic **Carousel**, located mid-Park at 64th Street. It dates from 1908 and used to stand in a Coney Island amusement park. You can still ride it, weather permitting (Apr–Oct daily 10am–6pm, Nov–Mar call for hours, tel: 212-452 0707).

On the park's west side, near 66th Street, is **Tavern on the Green**. The gardens and building are dazzling and house an information center and a restaurant serving local and artisanal food. Nearby is the **Sheep Meadow**, a popular spot for playing Frisbee and for sunbathing in summer; it is also a great place for a picnic. The sheep that used to graze here were originally housed in the Tavern on the Green building.

Right in the middle of the park, beginning at 66th Street, is the **Literary Walk**, lined with statues of writers you will, for the most part, recognize. The path leads up to the Mall, where there is a band shell, and ends at the **Bethesda Terrace and Fountain**, one of the park's best-known spots. On the lake is the Loeb Boathouse, where there is a café in addition to a good, though fairly expensive, restaurant. You can rent a boat or a bike near here in the summer.

To the east is the **Conservatory Water**, a pond where hobbyists sail model boats. At its northern end (at 74th Street) sits Central Park's most beloved sculpture, a bronze grouping of characters from Lewis Carroll's *Alice's Adventures in Wonderland*.

To the west is **Strawberry Fields**, a poignant memorial to John Lennon, who on December 8, 1980 was shot and killed outside the nearby Dakota apartment building at 72nd Street and Central Park West. The memorial features decorative mosaic pathways and a woodland walk.

Relaxing in Central Park, the lungs of Manhattan

North (at 80th Street) is the **Delacorte Theater**, best known as the stage for the summer's free Shakespeare in the Park productions.

In the center of the park is **Belvedere Castle ㉓**, which affords excellent views; inside is a nature center and weather station. From the Castle, you will be able to see the central part of the park, which features the **Great Lawn**, popular with sun worshippers. On the east side is the Metropolitan Museum of Art (see page 51), and just to the south is **Cleopatra's Needle** (at 81st Street), a 3,600-year-old obelisk that was a gift from Egypt in the 19th century.

North of here are several other notable features. The gravel path around the **Jacqueline Kennedy Onassis Reservoir** (mid-Park, north of 86th Street) is a favorite with joggers. The **North Meadow** (mid-Park, at 96th Street) is another open expanse, and often serves as the site of free concerts. At 104th Street is the **Conservatory Garden**. At the northern end of the park on the east side is the **Harlem Meer**, a lake.

UPPER WEST SIDE

Beginning at **Columbus Circle**, where Broadway and Eighth Avenue (thereafter renamed Central Park West) converge, the Upper West Side stretches north to Columbia University (about 110th Street);

The Dairy

You might want to drop in at the Dairy (mid-Park at 65th Street; Tue–Sat 10am–5pm), the Central Park visitors' center. The attractive Victorian Gothic structure was actually built as a dairy in 1870 in order to provide fresh milk to families. Today it displays a permanent exhibit on the park's history and design and provides visitors with brochures and information.

its western boundary is the Hudson River and Riverside Park; its eastern boundary is Central Park. Columbus Circle is invigorated by the towering Deutsche Bank Center that overlooks Central Park; the center includes The Shops at Columbus Circle shopping mall, the Mandarin Oriental Hotel, a collection of restaurants – including some of the biggest names in fine dining (including Thomas Keller's Per Se) – and the home of Jazz at Lincoln Center.

At 2 Columbus Circle is the **Museum of Arts and Design** (www.madmuseum.org; Tue–Sun 10am–6pm) and its collection of everything from teapots to antique quilts and rocking chairs.

LINCOLN CENTER

The cultural epicenter of the Upper West Side is the **Lincoln Center for the Performing Arts ㉔** (www.lincolncenter.org), which is bounded by 62nd and 66th streets (on the south and north), Amsterdam (the continuation of Tenth Avenue) on the west, and Columbus (the continuation of Ninth Avenue) on the east. The Center covers an area of 16 acres (7 hectares). The central plaza, a vast esplanade surrounding a fountain, acts as the focal point for the three main buildings. Built in 1960, the whole space is in the midst of a vast modernization program.

In the center is the **Metropolitan Opera House**

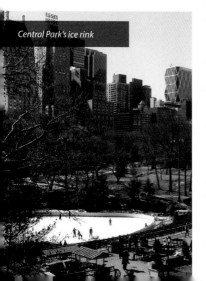
Central Park's ice rink

(the other 'Met'), home to the Metropolitan Opera. The opera house was designed by Wallace K. Harrison and completed in 1966. It can hold nearly 4,000 people. Two Chagall murals adorning the central lobby can be seen from the outside. To the left of the Met is the **David H. Koch Theater**, home of the New York City Ballet and sometimes the American Ballet Theater. Designed by architect Philip Johnson and built in 1964, it has a simple, stately facade complemented by a red-and-gold auditorium studded with crystal; the notoriously bad acoustics were upgraded through the installation of a modern sound system. To the right of the Met, opposite the David H. Koch Theater, is **David Geffen Hall**, completed in 1962, which is primarily used for music concerts.

Walkers in the park

Just behind David Geffen Hall, you can make out the outline of **Vivian Beaumont Theater**, the only uptown stage for Broadway plays. Across 65th Street is the **Walter Reade Theater**, where the Film Society of Lincoln Center screens movies.

Founded and established in 1961, the **American Folk Art Museum** (2 Lincoln Square; www.folkartmuseum.org; Wed–Sun 11.30am–6pm) celebrates the 'extraordinary accomplishments of ordinary people.' The museum has exhibits ranging from 18th- and 19th-century paintings, to quilts, contemporary sculpture, furniture and pottery.

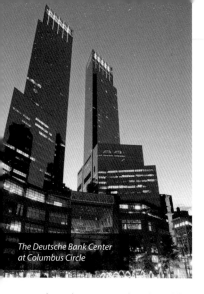
The Deutsche Bank Center at Columbus Circle

Farther back, but connected to Lincoln Center by a footbridge over West 65th Street, is the Juilliard School, one of the world's outstanding music conservatories.

Farther north are several interesting things to see. The Ansonia, at 2109 Broadway (73rd and 74th streets), is a notable Beaux-Arts apartment building. A little farther west, at the corner of 72nd and Central Park West, is the **Dakota**, which dates to 1884; it has been home to such rich and famous residents as John Lennon and Lauren Bacall and was the setting for the 1968 film *Rosemary's Baby*. John Lennon was murdered in of the building in 1980; his widow, Yoko Ono, still lives here.

A few blocks farther north, between 76th and 77th streets, is the **New York Historical Society** (www.nyhistory.org; Wed–Sun 11am–5pm, Fri until 8pm), the oldest museum in New York (the second-oldest in the US). In addition to documents and artifacts of historical interest, the Society's collection includes a collection of American fine and decorative arts.

NATURAL HISTORY MUSEUM

The huge building on Central Park West at 79th Street is the **American Museum of Natural History** ㉕ (www.amnh.org; daily 10am–5.45pm), another of New York's oldest museums, dating to 1869. Once considered a pretty stuffy place full of old dinosaur bones and dusty taxidermy displays, much of the museum has been reinvented over the past couple of decades and it is now one of the city's most popular collections; crowds are drawn to the **Hayden Planetarium**, the centerpiece of the Frederick Phineas and Sandra Priest Rose Center for Earth and Space. Its Journey to the Stars is an exciting and informative theatrical experience that introduces all ages to the creation of the universe and our solar system.

With tens of millions of specimens and artifacts, the museum is a repository for knowledge about virtually any aspect of earth's natural history and development. The creaking dioramas are still there and now seem quaint, but the refurbished parts of the museum have the most up-to-the-minute scientific information and wonderful state-of-the-art exhibitions. Examples of this are

Lincoln Center for the Performing Arts

the Fossil Halls – covering everything from dinosaurs to mammals – and the Hall of Biodiversity, which includes a life-size recreation of a rainforest.

Don't miss the full-size model of a blue whale, the Star of India (the largest sapphire that has ever been discovered), and the Barosaurus in the Theodore Roosevelt Rotunda on Central Park West: standing on its rear legs, this long-necked sauropod is the tallest free-standing dinosaur exhibit in the world.

Tours of the collection's highlights are given regularly throughout the day and there are always a few special exhibitions worth visiting. The museum also has a massive IMAX theater.

COLUMBIA UNIVERSITY AREA

Many visitors are surprised to find one of the largest neo-Gothic cathedrals in the world in New York City. The **Episcopal Cathedral Church of St John the Divine**, at Amsterdam Avenue and 112th Street (www.stjohndivine.org; Mon–Fri 9.30am–3pm, Sat 9.30am–5pm, Sun noon–5pm, see website for information on sightseeing tours), was begun in 1892 and is yet to be completed. The church is well known for its jazz and choral music series, in addition to its rotating art exhibits and festivals.

Columbia University

Beyond the cathedral, at 116th and Broadway, lies the campus of **Columbia University**. Founded in 1754 as King's College, Columbia is New York City's representative in the Ivy League. A private university, its schools of law and journalism and the teacher's college are widely recognized for their excellence. The School of Journalism is perhaps most famous for administering the Pulitzer Prizes. The campus itself is striking. Right across Broadway stands Barnard College, Columbia University's affiliated women's college.

Close by, in Riverside Park at West 122nd Street, is **Grant's Tomb** ❷❻, the mausoleum of Ulysses S. Grant. Here lies the commanding General of the Union Army in the Civil War and US President (1869–1877), alongside his wife, Julia Dent Grant. After the war, the general settled in New York City, worked on Wall Street and died in Upstate New York in July 1885. Administered by the National Park Service, the mausoleum, which is the biggest in the US, contains a museum devoted to Grant's life (https://www.nps.gov/gegr; visits Wed–Sun 10–11am, noon–1pm, 2–3pm, 4–5pm; visitors' center open Wed–Sun 9am–5pm).

HARLEM AND NORTH MANHATTAN

A major African-American cultural, spiritual and business center, **Harlem** continues to undergo an economic renaissance and rapid gentrification. It is a vital and varied community with rich, poor and middle-income sections, historical landmarks and attractive homes.

A popular way to see Harlem is on one of the hop-on-hop-off double-decker bus tours, or on a specialized tour that often includes lunch and a gospel music performance. Tours that include a Sunday church service are especially popular. For more information, see page 124.

Harlem begins north of Central Park at 110th Street and extends to 178th Street, bounded on the west by Morningside Heights and Washington Heights and on the north and east by the Harlem River, which connects the Hudson and East rivers. The neighborhood's main commercial center is 125th Street, where you'll find the historic **Apollo Theater** (253 West 125th Street; www.apollotheater.org).

AN HISTORIC DISTRICT

Founded by Dutch settlers, Harlem remained a village for a long time. As immigrants moved into the Lower East Side, many middle-class families moved north to Harlem. The influx of black families started around 1900 and reached its height around 1920, when the area became a cultural hub and home to prominent artists and writers associated with the Harlem Renaissance. Historic row houses of this period are preserved in the **St Nicholas Historic District** between Adam Clayton Powell, Jr. Boulevard and Frederick Douglass Boulevard on 138th and 139th streets.

There are several prominent cultural institutions in the area. The **Studio Museum in Harlem ㉗** (144 West 125th Street, at Lenox Avenue; www.studiomuseum.org; closed for renovation until 2024, see website for temporary location), is dedicated to African-American, Caribbean, and contemporary and traditional

HARLEM'S CHURCHES

Central Harlem is known for its beautiful churches. The Abyssinian Baptist Church at 132 Odell Clark Place (aka West 138th Street) was founded in 1808; its current Harlem home dates to 1923. Also in the area is the Mother AME Zion Church, at 146 West 137th Street, which is the oldest African-American church in New York. St Philip's Episcopal Church is a striking neo-Gothic building at 204 West 134th Street.

African art. At Malcolm X Boulevard and 135th Street, the **Schomburg Center for Research in Black Culture** (www.nypl.org/locations/schomburg; Tue–Sat 10am–5pm), a branch of the New York Public Library and an art museum, has one of the world's most important collections covering black history and African-American culture.

Historic Harlem

North of Harlem is the **Hamilton Grange National Memorial** (www.nps.gov/hagr) which was the early 19th-century home of Founding Father Alexander Hamilton. The house was renovated and moved to St Nicholas Park in 2011. The surrounding area, roughly between St Nicholas and Edgecombe avenues and 143rd to 155th streets, was once Hamilton's farm. It is now known as **Hamilton Heights** and is home to a historic area that includes the Sugar Hill row houses. The **Morris-Jumel Mansion** and gardens (1765) at 65 Jumel Terrace (near 162nd street) exhibits period furniture (www.morrisjumel.org; Tue–Sun 10am–4pm, Sat–Sun until 5pm).

The 1908 Beaux-Arts style **Audubon Terrace** complex, on Broadway between 155th and 156th streets, is home to two cultural institutions. The **American Academy of Arts and Letters** (www.artsandletters.org) has seasonal exhibitions, but is otherwise not open to the public. The **Hispanic Society of America** has a permanent collection that includes rare books and manuscripts and works by Goya and El Greco. Entrance to the society's library and museum is free to the public (www.hispanicsociety.org; closed for renovation).

WASHINGTON HEIGHTS

Above Harlem, Manhattan narrows to a little sliver made up of **Washington Heights** and Inwood. Both are primarily residential neighborhoods, but there are a couple of interesting attractions. Washington Heights was long known as a drug-seller's haven, but it has cleaned up its act and is welcoming a diverse set of new residents who are joining the large Dominican population.

THE CLOISTERS

Beyond Washington Heights is **Fort Tryon Park**, 66 acres (26 hectares) of landscaped and terraced hills, which begins at 190th Street. From the subway stop (A line), it's possible to walk through the park to **The Cloisters** ㉘ (www.metmuseum.org; Thu–Tue 10am–4.30pm). Part of the Metropolitan Museum (your admission to the Met also gives you same-day admission here), this branch is devoted to Medieval art and architecture. It is built around parts of several actual cloisters and other medieval structures transported from Europe. The views of the Hudson River from the outdoor terraces are

Eating in Harlem

If you yearn for something to eat in Harlem, there are many good choices. The place that says Harlem for most people is Sylvia's (328 Lenox Avenue, at 127th Street, tel: 212-996 0660; www.sylviasrestaurant.com), where you can sample typical South Carolina fare; its Sunday gospel brunch is especially popular. Another popular eatery is Amy Ruth's (113 West 116th Street, tel: 212-280 8779; www.amyruths.com).

breathtaking, and the gardens provide a great place to sit in reflective solitude.

Housed within The Cloisters are several genuine masterpieces, including the wood sculpture *Enthroned Virgin and Child*, a set of 'nine heroes' tapestries, a 12th-century carved ivory cross, and the museum's most popular holding, a set of tapestries depicting the *Hunt of the Unicorn*.

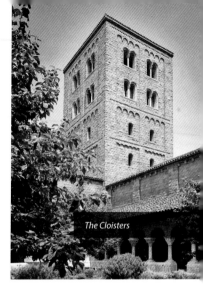
The Cloisters

Not far away is the **Dyckman Farmhouse Museum** at 4881 Broadway (www.dyckmanfarmhouse.org; Fri and Sat 10am–4pm, with exceptions), the only remaining Dutch colonial farmhouse in Manhattan. If you are in the area, it's worth a detour.

OTHER NEIGHBORHOODS

THE LOWER EAST SIDE

At the turn of the 20th century, the Lower East Side of Manhattan was the most densely populated place in the US, home to around half a million Russian and Eastern European Jewish immigrants. The remnants of the old Jewish neighborhood are located on the northeast side of Chinatown, beyond Hester Street, the site of the Jewish market at the end of the 19th century. Follow Hester Street east and then walk north along **Orchard Street**, and you'll see a

The Lower East Side
Tenement Museum

shadow of the market's heyday mixed in with hip eateries and new clubs.

In this New World ghetto, the cornerstone of the economy was the 'needle trade.' Working conditions and pay were appalling. Those who didn't toil in the garment factories often worked as peddlers or pushcart vendors, selling produce or cheap clothing in the markets on Hester Street and Orchard Street. The **Lower East Side Tenement Museum**  at 97 Orchard Street offers an introduction to this area. The 19th-century tenement can be seen by guided tour only, and visitors view restored apartments of immigrant families in the tenement at different historical periods. Tours start from the Visitor Center, across the road at 103 Orchard Street (www.tenement. org; Mon–Thu 10am–5pm, Fri–Sun 10am–6pm, tour times vary; advance ticket purchase strongly recommended).

THE BOWERY AND NOLITA

The Bowery is located on the eastern border of the Lower East Side. Once notorious as New York City's skid row, the Bowery and surrounding neighborhoods are filling up with luxury condominium buildings at a rapid pace. The Whole Foods Market (www. wholefoodsmarket.com) at the corner of Bowery and Houston is always busy and a good place to take a break and grab a snack from a large selection of prepared foods. On the Bowery across from Prince Street is the **New Museum**, opened in 2007 (www.newmuseum.org; Tue–Sun 11am–6pm, Thu until 9pm) and the only one in the city devoted exclusively to contemporary art. The blocks surrounding nearby St Patrick's Old Cathedral (263 Mulberry St, at Prince St; www.oldcathedral.org) were rechristened Nolita ("North of Little Italy") by savvy real-estate developers in the late 1990s. Stylish shop-owners are the newest variety of immigrant here, as numerous tiny boutiques have taken over former Italian haunts.

CHINATOWN

Of all the ethnic neighborhoods that were established on New York's Lower East Side, it is the Chinese enclave that has continued to thrive. The narrow shops sell ivory and jade jewelry, as well as bootleg designer watches and the usual souvenirs; grocers display exotic Chinese produce; and the area's innumerable restaurants feature a huge range of regional specialties. The earliest Chinese arrivals came here in the 19th century, after the California Gold Rush and the boom of railway construction. These days, the majority of Chinese immigrants actually live in Queens and Brooklyn, but many still work and play in bustling **Chinatown**, a loosely defined area embracing Canal Street, Chatham Square, and Mott Street. At 215 Centre Street is the **Museum of Chinese in America ㉚** (www.mocanyc.org; Thu–Sun 11am–6pm, Thu until 9pm). In addition to cultural programs and exhibitions, the museum conducts walking tours of the neighborhood.

Near Chatham Square, at the corner of Division Street and Bowery, stands a 1983 bronze statue of Confucius. South of the square, a few steps down St. James Place, are some of New York's oldest monuments, barely a dozen tombstones, the remnants of the **Shearith Israel Cemetery**, founded here in 1656 by New York's first immigrants, Spanish and Portuguese Jews.

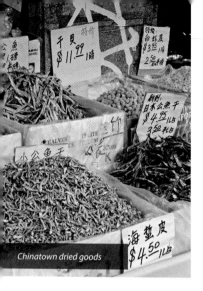
Chinatown dried goods

LITTLE ITALY

'Little' is certainly the operative word here, as this area has now been largely subsumed by Chinatown. The stretch of Mulberry Street from Canal to Grand is still home to several Italian restaurants and expensive coffee bars. In the summer, especially on weekends, it is a pleasant place to stroll, buy a souvenir, and have a plate of pasta and a glass of house wine al fresco. There are still some good 'old world' bakeries and grocers here, though some of them, too, are now Chinese.

The district is at its liveliest during the ten-day Feast of San Gennaro in early September (see page 98). But if you find yourself in the neighborhood, you might want to take a stroll over to the old **Police Headquarters** at the corner of Centre and Grand streets; this is the building in which Theodore Roosevelt served as New York City's police commissioner. The inhabitants are now the tenants of the luxury condominiums created in the late 1980s.

SOHO AND TRIBECA

SoHo (South of Houston) is the area bound by Houston Street, Broadway, Canal Street, and the Hudson River. It has become the Village's chic southern neighbor, with expensive cafes, restaurants, art galleries, and shops selling the very latest in fashion and housewares.

Its history has followed the pattern of Greenwich Village. Artists who couldn't afford the rents after the Village's commercialization moved south to the derelict lofts and warehouse floors of the then industrial district. The most successful were able to install kitchens, bathrooms, and comfortable interiors, while others made do with bare walls and floors for the sake of ample space and light. Now the same lofts sell in the multi-million dollar range.

The main things to do here are to browse in the handful of remaining galleries, stop and relax at the many outdoor cafés and restaurants, and shop. There are plenty of interesting smaller bou-tiques located on side streets off Broadway, which is home to many big-name designers and chain stores.

West Broadway is the quintessential SoHo street. Here you'll find the choicest boutiques and galleries. After SoHo became too expensive, the artists moved out, many heading southwest to the derelict warehouses of the **Tribeca** (Triangle Below Canal) neighborhood, which in its turn has inevitably seen the opening of upscale restau-rants and trendy boutiques. As those rents began to soar, many of the artists migrated to Brooklyn and Queens and the art dealers moved to Chelsea.

The colors of Little Italy

GREENWICH VILLAGE

'The Village,' as **Greenwich Village** is usually called, has been separate, casual, and very different from the rest of the city ever since its beginnings. In colonial times it really was a distinct village called Greenwich, which became a neighborhood of conservative Georgian brick houses and carriage barns in back-alley mews. A few of these houses remain, mostly on **Bedford Street** and the streets around it, but conservative the Village isn't. It got its bohemian reputation after World War I, when artists and writers moved here for the area's cheap lodgings, inexpensive restaurants and speakeasies. Later, the Village became the center for New York's LGBTQ+ community, which to a large degree has now moved north to Chelsea.

The Village is roughly the area from 14th Street down to Houston and west of Broadway. The area's heart is **Washington Square Park ㉛**, the de facto campus quad for **New York University**, which controls much of the real estate east of Sixth Avenue and south of 14th Street to Houston. The park's famous arch was designed by architect Stanford White and erected in 1889 to mark the centenary of George Washington's inauguration as president.

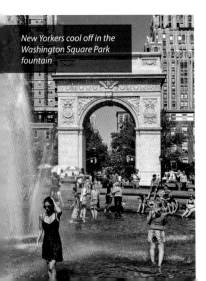

New Yorkers cool off in the Washington Square Park fountain

Bleecker Street with its craft and curio shops, antique stores, cafés, and tiny restaurants has long been the main shopping strip of the neighborhood. The area's highest concentration of LGBTQ+-owned businesses and bars is still found on **Christopher Street**, west of Seventh Avenue South. The Stonewall Inn, at 53 Christopher Street (now an official National Monument), stands on the site of the original Stonewall Inn, which was the site of the riots in 1969 that led to the modern gay rights movement. You may wish to make at least two trips to the Village; by day to shop and see the sights, and at night to catch the atmosphere, have dinner, and hit one of the jazz clubs or bars.

De Niro's Tribeca

Tribeca's expensive loft-style real estate is home to many high-profile New Yorkers. Perhaps the district's most ardent resident-supporter is actor Robert De Niro. He opened his restaurant Tribeca Grill, which is still going strong, and instituted the Tribeca Film Festival.

EAST VILLAGE

A separate community, the **East Village** extends east from Broadway to Avenue D and the East River. Less affluent than Greenwich Village to the west, this neighborhood has nevertheless fallen victim to plenty of gentrification and is probably the hippest place in Manhattan. You will find eclectic, edgy boutiques, restaurants, and shops that can't afford the other downtown rents. If there is any real bohemian spirit left in Manhattan, it may be here. Walk down St Mark's Place or Avenue A, the liveliest streets, or people-watch in Tompkins Square.

On Lafayette Street, just to the south of Cooper Square, stands the building that once housed the first public library of New York. Nowadays it is the seat of **The Public Theater**, which actually contains several theaters and is the host of Shakespeare in the Park. Joe's Pub, off the main lobby, is a celebrated venue for live music and performance. Nearby is the Great Hall of the Cooper Union, the

The Gay Liberation statue in Christopher Park

center of the once-free university established by Peter Cooper in 1859.

Those interested in historic buildings might stop by **St Mark's-in-the-Bowery**, built in 1799 on the very spot where the Stuyvesant family chapel once stood (at 10th Street at Second Avenue). It is now a charming church with some noteworthy stained-glass windows and a spirited congregation, often hosting music or dance performances. The tomb of Dutch governor Peter Stuyvesant lies here.

MEATPACKING DISTRICT AND CHELSEA

The northwest corner of Greenwich Village from West 14th Street to Gansevoort Street is a designated historic district of cobbled streets and warehouses. Home to a meat market during the last century, the area is now awash with trendy boutiques, restaurants, bars, clubs and hotels.

The **High Line** ㉜ (www.thehighline.org; daily June–Sept 7am–11pm, Apr–May and Oct–Nov until 10pm, Dec–Mar until 7pm) is a major public park built on elevated railroad tracks. These tracks were originally constructed in the 1930s to lift freight trains off the streets of Manhattan. They have been converted into a beautifully landscaped walkway that stretches 1.45 miles (2.3km) from Gansevoort Street to West 34th Street and 10th Avenue, with multiple entrances and exits. The High Line ends at the Hudson Yards development of skyscrapers, where the Edge (www.edgenyc.com/en) offers sensational panoramic views 100 stories up.

Housed in a striking building by architect Renzo Piano back in the Meatpacking District, the excellent **Whitney Museum of American Art** ❸ (www.whitney.org; Mon and Wed–Thu 10.30am–6pm, Fri 10.30am–10pm, Sat and Sun 11am–6pm) was originally founded by Gertrude Vanderbilt Whitney, an artist from one of New York's wealthiest families. It is one of the few museums that is dedicated solely to American art and that seeks out works from alternative media, such as film and video. By focusing its collection on contemporary American artists (both those of Ms. Whitney's era and those of today), it has gone a long way toward changing attitudes about the diversity and strength of the country's art. The permanent collection includes works by such artists as Andy Warhol, Alexander Calder, Georgia O'Keefe, Jackson Pollock, Jasper Johns,

VILLAGE VOICES

Since the Art Nouveau period, Greenwich Village has been one big 'village of genius' and home of the artistic avant-garde. The radical paper *Masses*, whose contributors included Maxim Gorki, Bertrand Russell, and John Reed, had its offices here. In 1914, Gertrude Vanderbilt Whitney opened a gallery and provided a platform for contemporary artists, much of whose work was highly controversial. In 1916, members of the Playwrights' Theater settled on MacDougal Street and soon achieved fame, Eugene O'Neill among them.

After World War II the Bohemian image of 'the Village' persisted. In the 1950s, the beatnik movement flowered (Jack Kerouac and Allen Ginsberg); in the 1960s and early '70s the area was home to hippies and anti-Vietnam war activists (Abbie Hoffman and Jerry Rubin).

and Mark Rothko. Curators continue to build and show works by living artists.

The Chelsea neighborhood between 14th and 39th streets, west of Sixth Avenue, is thriving after many years of decline. This is one of the trendiest LGBTQ+ neighborhoods in Manhattan. Stroll up Eighth Avenue, where you'll find gay bars and boutiques, as well as all sorts of restaurants. The **Joyce Theater** (www.joyce.org), at 19th Street, is one of the city's main modern dance venues. On 23rd Street, between Seventh and Eighth avenues, sits the famous (and infamous) **Chelsea Hotel**, with its distinctive wrought iron balconies. The former home to artists, rock stars and assorted sketchy characters, it gradually reopened in 2022 following extensive renovation. Along the Hudson River, the Chelsea Piers (www.chelseapiers.com) serves up six blocks of sports and entertainment from 17th to 23rd streets.

Seventh Avenue is quieter, but you will still find many restaurants and stores. Sixth Avenue from 18th to 23rd streets was once known as the 'Ladies Mile.' For many years, the massive storefronts stood derelict; now they are inhabited by box stores like Old Navy and Bed, Bath, and Beyond.

Chelsea has long superseded SoHo as the place for **contemporary art**. There are close to 200 galleries on the far west side between Tenth and Twelfth avenues.

Chilling out on the High Line

EXCURSIONS TO THE OUTER BOROUGHS

BROOKLYN

Brooklyn, which actually has a larger population than Manhattan, is one of America's largest urban centers. It is well worth a trip over the East River. **Brooklyn Heights**, the neighborhood closest to Manhattan, is easy to reach. Take subway lines 2 or 3 to Clark Street, or cross the Brooklyn Bridge on foot from the east side of City Hall Park (see page 33); the view is unparalleled.

Rising above the East River, the Heights is an attractive area of 19th-century brownstones and picturesque streets, long popular with writers and artists. The **Promenade** (three blocks down Clark Street from the bridge) is an esplanade with an impressive view, including both the Manhattan skyline and the Statue of Liberty. Late afternoon is a good time to go, when the towers of Lower Manhattan start to glow in the light of the setting sun. At the end of the Promenade, walk south along shady Hicks Street, in a quarter that has changed little since 1860.

If you are interested in subways and how they are run, then a trip to the **New York Transit Museum** is in order (www.nytransit-museum.org; Tue–Fri 10am–4pm, Sat–Sun 11am–5pm). Housed in an authentic 1930s subway station at the corner of Boerum Place and Schermerhorn Street, the museum has a great variety of exhibits, many with interactive components. They also have an annex museum in Grand Central Terminal (see page 44).

The **Brooklyn Museum of Art** ❹ (www.brooklynmuseum.org; 200 Eastern Parkway; Wed–Sun 11am–6pm, Fri and Sat until 8pm, with exceptions) is the second-largest museum in New York, with exceptional collections of Egyptian, Asian, Persian, and pre-Columbian art. The permanent collection includes more than 1.5 million objects, and the African art collection is one of the largest and most important in the United States. Take the 2 or 3 subway to Eastern Parkway-Brooklyn Museum.

Adjacent to the museum is the **Brooklyn Botanic Garden (www.bbg.org)**. Not to be confused with the larger New York Botanical Garden in the Bronx, it is nevertheless a peaceful place to stroll. Nearby is **Prospect Park**, a 526-acre (212-hectare) urban oasis designed by Frederick Law Olmsted and Calvert Vaux (who designed Central Park). A combined visit to the museum, botanic garden, and park is a nice way to spend a day.

THE BRONX

For a while now, the **Bronx** has had a reputation for crime and urban decay. While there are certainly parts of the Bronx where this is still true, visitors who haven't been here lately will be surprised.

Waterfall in Brooklyn Botanic Garden

Several attractions make it worth a special trip to New York's only borough on the US mainland.

One such attraction is the **Bronx Zoo** 🖲 (www.bronxzoo.com; Apr–Oct Mon–Fri 10am–5pm, Sat–Sun 10am–5.30pm, Nov–Mar daily 10am–4.30pm). At its most inviting from May through October, when all of the sections are open, the zoo has over 10,000 animals from over 700 species. At the Congo Gorilla Forest you

Siberian tiger at the Bronx Zoo

get to meet the zoo's gorillas up close. Though they are behind glass, there is still a lot of interaction with the crowd. Other popular exhibits are the Wild Asia monorail (where you can see tigers), JungleWorld, the World of Birds, Children's Zoo, the 4-D Theater, and, in the summer, the Butterfly Garden. There is an extra fee for entry into most of these special rides and attractions, or you can purchase a Total Experience ticket that will give you access to everything.

To get to the zoo, take the 2 or 5 subway to East Tremont/West Farms Square. When you exit at street level, walk straight ahead (follow train uptown) for two and a half blocks on Boston Road to the zoo's Asia gate entrance (Gate A). Alternatively, you can take Metro North from Grand Central to Fordham station, then catch the BX9 bus to the Southern Boulevard Entrance. You can also take the BXM11 Express Bus from Midtown, which runs up Madison Avenue. The Bronx Zoo is the first stop after 99th Street.

Adjacent to the zoo is the 250-acre (100-hectare) **New York Botanical Garden** (www.nybg.org; Tue–Sun 10am–6pm, closes at 5pm in winter, with exceptions). Highlights include specialty gardens, an orchid collection, a 40-acre (16-hectare) uncut, almost virgin forest, and the Enid A. Haupt Conservatory. Children will enjoy learning about plants and nature in the adventure garden. The visitor center includes a shop, café, and visitor orientation area. To get there, take Metro North from Grand Central to the New York Botanical Garden stop.

QUEENS

The most diverse borough of the five that make up New York, Queens has several attractions of interest. During the silent movie era, Queens was the equivalent of today's Hollywood – the

MoMA PS1, Queens

center of the motion-picture industry – and movies and TV shows are still made at the Kaufman Astoria Studios here. Located in the studio complex, on 35th Avenue at 36th Street in Astoria, the **American Museum of the Moving Image** (www. movingimage.us; Wed–Thu 10.30am–5pm, Fri 10.30am– 8pm, Sat–Sun 10.30am–6pm) celebrates this early movie history and explores the art, technique, and technology of film, television, and digital media, examining their impact on society. To reach the museum, take the R subway to Steinway Street or the N to 36 Avenue (Astoria) and walk.

> ### Yankee tours
>
> Baseball fans may be interested to know that you can take a 60-min tour of Yankee Stadium, in the Bronx, during baseball season (May–September), but this is only permitted on days when the team is not playing at home. You must make an advance ticket reservation through Ticketmaster or visit www. mlb.com.

In Long Island City, just across from midtown Manhattan, is the **MoMA PS1** (22–25 Jackson Avenue at 46th Street; www.moma. org/ps1; Thu–Mon noon–6pm, Sat until 8pm), the largest contemporary art museum in New York and well worth a visit. It's the second location of the Museum of Modern Art, beside midtown Manhattan. To get there, take the E subway to Court Square/23rd Street or the 7 to 45th Road/Courthouse Square.

Also in Long Island City is the **Noguchi Museum ㊱** (9–01 33rd Road, at Vernon Boulevard; www.noguchi.org; Wed–Sun 11am– 6pm), created by Japanese-American sculptor, furniture designer and landscape architect Isamu Noguchi to house a comprehensive collection of his modernist and earlier works. A former factory, this has been renovated into a contemplative space with tranquil gardens.

A shopkeeper presides over traditional foodstuffs in Chinatown

THINGS TO DO

SHOPPING

If you can't afford to buy, you can always window-shop, a pastime in itself. Virtually anything is available in Manhattan for a price, which is sometimes, though certainly not always, a bargain.

WHEN AND WHERE TO SHOP

If you are looking for inexpensive New York souvenirs, avoid Midtown and the areas around major tourist attractions, such as the Empire State Building. Instead, try 14th Street, particularly between Fifth and Sixth avenues, as well as Chinatown, especially the north side of Canal and the blocks on either side of Mulberry. Greenwich Village can still be an interesting place to shop; browse the quirky smaller stores along Bleecker Street and shop for records, books and vintage clothes. SoHo, a major weekend destination for area shoppers, is the home of a few fine art galleries and plenty of designer-clothing and home-furnishings stores. There are also upmarket boutiques and thrift shops selling designer gems in Chelsea, and an eclectic variety of retailers and great vintage shops in the East Village.

The reliable shopping neighborhoods have always been Fifth Avenue above 50th Street and Madison Avenue from Midtown to the Upper East Side. For decades the former was very chic, but is now increasingly predictable and loaded with chain and theme stores; the latter is home to some luxurious, high-end shops. The Upper West Side's shopping destination is the **Time Warner Center** overlooking Central Park, where more than 40 high-end retailers take up four floors at the base of the building on Columbus Circle.

WHAT TO BUY

Art and antiques. Art galleries and antiques shops are found throughout the city. The largest concentrations are along East 57th Street and up Madison Avenue to 84th Street. A movement away from SoHo, where there are still some galleries, has led to a boom in west Chelsea (between West 19th Street and West 27th Street, around 10th and 11th avenues). There are some good antique stores on Bleecker Street, west of Christopher Street in Greenwich Village, as well as clustered around 10th and 11th streets at University Place. One institution worth visiting for its wide range of choices is the **Manhattan Art and Antiques Center** (1050 Second Avenue at 56th Street; www.the-maac.com), which boasts some 100 galleries selling ceramics, crystal, and assorted bric-a-brac.

For flea markets, try the **Chelsea Flea** (www.chelseaflea.com; 29 West 25th Street, between Fifth and Sixth avenues, Sat–Sun 8am–4pm) featuring 50 to 60 vendors selling antiques, collectibles, decorative arts, vintage clothing and jewelry. The Brooklyn Flea (www.brooklynflea.com) manages the Chelsea market, but in the summer (Apr–Oct) gets going with a couple of extra locations across the East River: Saturdays in Williamsburg (51 North Sixth Street), Sundays in Dumbo (Manhattan Bridge Archway, 80 Pearl Street). It also runs the wildly popular Smorgasburg (www.smorgasburg.com) food market in Williamsburg and Prospect Park in Brooklyn.

Clothing. You really can find bargains among the prodigious array of clothes in the department stores, especially during end-of-season sales. But it would be a shame to limit your search

---

Macy's, the giant

Macy's, established in New York City in 1858, is America's largest store, at 2.5 million sq ft (230,000 sq m). It stocks more than 500,000 items.

to the bigger stores. Head to Madison Avenue above 60th Street for high-fashion boutiques; to SoHo (expensive) and the East Village (less expensive) for more daring designs; to Fifth Avenue for reliable luxury labels; and to the Meatpacking District for hip party-wear. For used and vintage designer clothing try Beacon's Closet (www.beaconscloset.com), which has its main branch at 74 Guernsey Street, Greenpoint (Brooklyn), and smaller

Bloomingdale's

branches in Park Slope (92 5th Avenue) and Greenwich Village (10 West 13th Street).

Computers and electronics. Approach the so-called 'discount' electronics stores of Midtown with a critical eye; sales techniques can be high-pressure and the prices are not always as good as you might think. Many of the dealers are reputable, however, and real bargains can be found if you know what you are looking for. New Yorkers still shop at **Best Buy** (1280 Lexington Avenue; www.bestbuy.com) or **B&H Photo** (420 Ninth Avenue at 34th Street; www.bhphotovideo.com), where you can find absolutely everything and the staff are knowledgeable. Computer stores are concentrated on Fifth Avenue, above 20th Street; they include the Microsoft Experience Center at 677 Fifth Avenue and the **Apple Store** at 767 Fifth Avenue (see page 42).

Department stores. Macy's (34th and Broadway) and **Bloomingdale's** (59th and Lexington, and the SoHo location, at

504 Broadway) have everything; **Saks Fifth Avenue** (at 50th) is strictly high fashion for ladies who lunch and their gentlemen, as is **Bergdorf Goodman** (57th and Fifth Avenue). Nordstrom's glossy modern store at 57th and Broadway features seven floors of curated clothing, shoes and accessories.

Jewelry. Hit the Diamond District on West 47th for all prices and styles, but not always bargains; Fifth Avenue above 50th Street is the location for the high-end jewelers (Cartier, Tiffany, Harry Winston, Bulgari, Swarovski and Van Cleef & Arpels). Small boutiques in SoHo, Greenwich Village, and the East Village are good for hand-made originals.

Music and books. With the advent of online retailing, the big record stores have shut down. The city does still have some small, independent music stores with dedicated music lovers who keep them going, like **Academy Records** (415 East 12th Street; www.academy-lps.com), **A1 Record Shop** (439 East 6th Street), and **Generation Records** (210 Thompson Street between Bleecker and 4th Street; www.generationrecords.com).

MUSEUM SHOPS

American Folk Art Museum. 2 Lincoln Square; www.folkart-museum.org. Rural crafts and toys from around the country.

Metropolitan Museum of Art Gift Shop. In the museum on Fifth Avenue and also at Rockefeller Center at 15 West 49th Street; www.store.metmuseum.org. Art books, posters, jewelry, reproductions.

The MoMA Design Store. 18 Spring Street, 11 West 53rd Street and 44 West 53rd Street; www.momastore.org. Designer furniture and household articles (see page 43).

The Museum of the City of New York. Fifth Avenue at 103rd Street; www.mcny.org. The place to go to find old prints of the city.

In the book realm, **Barnes and Noble** has superstores catering to the masses (97 Warren Street, Union Square North, 555 Fifth Avenue and three more). A fixture on the independent bookstore scene is the excellent **McNally Jackson** (52 Prince Street at Mulberry; www.mcnallyjackson.com) in Nolita (and three other branches). Specialty bookstores all over the city cater to such tastes as theater (**Drama Book Shop** at 266

Strand Book Store

West 39th Street; www.dramabookshop.com), mysteries (**The Mysterious Bookshop** at 58 Warren Street; www.mysterious-bookshop.com), science fiction and comics (**Forbidden Planet**, 832 Broadway at 13th Street; www.fpnyc.com), and art (MoMA or any museum store). Young readers will love Books of Wonder (42 West 17th Street; https://booksofwonder.com). For used books and out-of-print titles, head for **Strand Book Store** (Broadway at 12th Street; www.strandbooks.com).

New York originals. Zabar's (Broadway between 80th and 81st; www.zabars.com) and **Chelsea Market** (75 Ninth Ave, between 15th and 16th streets; www.chelseamarket.com) are fancy-food heavens. Folks come from all over the world to shop at **Paper Source** (75 Fifth Avenue). Honestly, if **M&J Trimming** (Sixth Avenue between 37th and 38th; www.mjtrim.com) doesn't have the ribbon, button or rhinestone you're looking for, it probably doesn't exist.

ENTERTAINMENT

They don't call New York the city that never sleeps for nothing. Whether you are interested in theater, the performing arts, a hot dance club, or just a quiet drink, you will have plenty of opportunities to have fun once the sun goes down. There is no way to cover the entire New York nightlife scene in these few pages. Luckily, there are plenty of resources for finding out what's going on either before you go, or once you have arrived in New York. The best places to find out what's going on are the Friday or Sunday *New York Times* (for mainstream events; www.nytimes.com), *The New Yorker or New York* magazines (good for arts and more sophisticated clubs and bars; www.newyorker.com and www.nymag.com), the *Village Voice* (an alternative online magazine, especially strong on music; www.villagevoice.com), or *Time Out New York* (online at www.timeout.com/newyork).

DISCOUNT THEATER TICKETS

Discount theater tickets (up to 50 percent off) for same-day performances can be purchased at two TKTS locations in Manhattan (www.tdf.org/nyc/7/TKTS-ticket-booths). The most popular is "under the red steps" in Father Duffy Square at 47th Street, which sells evening tickets daily after 3pm and matinee tickets after 11am on Wed, Sat and Sun. The other location is at Lincoln Center in the David Rubenstein Atrium at 61 West 62nd Street, which sells same day matinee and evening performances, plus next day matinees (Mon–Sat noon–7pm and Sun noon–5pm). Both of them accept credit cards, cash, or TKTS gift certificates. Note that the TKTS booths at South Street Seaport and in Brooklyn closed permanently during the Covid-19 pandemic, but check the website for updates.

Tickets to most events can be purchased from Ticketmaster, which charges a hefty service charge on top of the cost of the ticket itself. However, it is possible to purchase same-day tickets for Broadway and off-Broadway musicals and plays at substantial discounts.

Theater in the West Village

THEATER

One of the most popular activities for visitors is to take in a **Broadway** or **off-Broadway** show. Broadway theaters are concentrated in the Times Square area, but smaller off-Broadway houses are located all over town. Tickets for current hits must be booked ahead, sometimes months ahead. Curtain times are generally 8pm for evening performances, 2pm for matinees, which are usually on Wednesday, Saturday, and Sunday. Be prepared for a shock; the top shows charge well over $100 for their best seats, and American theaters often do not follow the lead of other countries by charging much less for the less desirable seats.

CLASSICAL MUSIC AND DANCE

New York has a particularly vibrant and diverse music scene, offering every kind of style imaginable, from opera and classical music to jazz, pop, blues, country, world, and reggae. Admission to many concerts is free: the summer concerts in Central Park, for instance, or the lunch-time concerts held in the Financial District and midtown.

New York City's two major opera companies are the **Metropolitan Opera** and the **New York City Opera** (www.met-opera.org and www.nycopera.com). The Met performs at Lincoln Center, while the City Opera performs at different venues around town. If you want to see world-famous artists, go to the Met, but the City Opera also produces some fine work. As for classical music concerts, you are likely to find a dozen or so scheduled for a single evening; often at **Carnegie Hall** (57th Street and Seventh Avenue; www.carnegiehall.org).

You will have more chances to see good dance performances in New York than in almost any other city in the world; from the **American Ballet Theater** and **New York City Ballet** (both at Lincoln Center; www.abt.org and www.nycballet.com), to modern and contemporary dance companies, many of which present their seasons at the **Joyce Theater** on Eighth Avenue (at 19th Street; www.joyce.org) and at **New York City Center** on Seventh Avenue (at 55th Street; www.nycitycenter.org). One should not forget such notable companies as those of Alvin Ailey (www.alvinailey.org), the Dance Theater of Harlem (www.dancetheatreofharlem.org), Martha Graham (www.marthagraham.org), Mark Morris (www.markmorrisdancegroup.org), and Paul Taylor (www.paultaylordance.org).

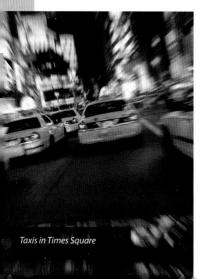

Taxis in Times Square

FILM

There are hundreds of mainstream movie screens in New York, but you will also have the chance to see many films that might not make it to your local multiplex. **MoMA**, the **Walter Reade Theater** at Lincoln Center, **Anthology Film Archive in the East Village** (www.anthologyfilmarchives.org), and the **Museum of the Moving Image** (www.movingimage.us) in Queens all have ongoing film series, mostly revivals of classic and art films. Other places to find movies that you might not otherwise see are: **Film Forum** (209 West Houston, between Sixth Avenue and Varick; www.filmforum.org); **New Plaza Cinema** (Broadway between 62nd and 63rd, https://new-plazacinema.com); the **Quad Cinema** (34 West 13th Street, between Fifth and Sixth avenues; www.quadcinema.com); the IFC Center **(323 6th Avenue; www.ifccenter.com)** and the **Angelika Film Center** (Houston and Mercer streets; www.angelikafilmcenter.com).

DANCE CLUBS

The thing to keep in mind about dance clubs in New York is that clubs can be quite different depending on when and where you go. Among the hundreds of ever-changing venues (and themes), you might consider trendy (**Marquee**, 289 Tenth Avenue between 26th and 27th; www.taogroup.com/venues/marquee-new-york) or house (**Schimanski**, 54 North 11th Street, Brooklyn; www.schiman-skinyc.com). There is also always the unapologetically chintzy mega-aclub **Webster Hall** (125 East 11th Street; www.websterhall.com).

CABARETS AND JAZZ CLUBS

New York is perhaps the center of world jazz. Listen to Jazz at **Iridium** (1650 Broadway at 51st Street; www.theiridium.com), the **Village Vanguard** (178 Seventh Avenue South; www.villa-gevanguard.com), the Blue Note (131 West 3rd Street; www.blue-notejazz.com/newyork), or **Birdland** (315 West 44th Street; www.

Serving cocktails at the Brass Monkey Bar

birdlandjazz.com). Some other places where you can hear good music while you drink and/or dine include **Joe's Pub** (in the Public Theater, Lafayette Street at Astor Place; www.publictheater.org/programs/joes-pub), or **Café Carlyle** (35 East 76th Street; www.cafecarlylenewyork.com), where long-time regular Woody Allen often performs on clarinet.

BARS

Hotel bars can be pretty swanky in New York. You will find popular ones at the **Shoreham**, **Baccarat**, and **Standard** hotels, as well as Bemelmans Bar at the Carlyle and Bar Pleiades at the Surrey. The lobby bars at the **Royalton** and **Four Seasons** hotels are fashionable places to meet. **Monkey Bar** at the **Hotel Elysée** (60 East 54th Street; www.elyseehotel.com) and the **King Cole Bar** in the **St Regis Hotel** (2 East 55th Street) are celebrated destinations.

Venture to the East Village, and you will find a good variety of bars: old-fashioned (**McSorley's Old Ale House** at 15 East 7th Street; www.mcsorleysoldalehouse.nyc), relaxed (**Von** at 3 Bleecker Street; www.vonbar.com), underground (**Raines Law Room** at 48 West 17th Street; www.raineslawroom.com), and fun (**Otto's Shrunken Head** at 538 East 14th Street; www.ottosshrunkenhead.com). Greenwich Village and the West Village offer a full range, from the cocktail oasis (**Little Branch** at 20 Seventh Avenue South at St Luke's Place) to the cozy beer-lovers' bar (**Blind Tiger Ale House** at 281

Bleecker Street at Jones Street; www.blindtigeralehouse.com) to the speakeasy-esque (**Employees Only** at 510 Hudson Street; www.employeesonlynyc.com). Chelsea offers the whole gamut from gay with sports (**Gym** at 167 Eighth Avenue; www.gymsportsbar.com) to gay without attitude (**Barracuda** at 275 West 22nd Street).

Then there are bars for everyone, such as the **Brass Monkey Bar** in the Meatpacking District (55 Little West 12th Street; www.brassmonkeynyc.com), a large but relaxing place to enjoy a beer. Tried-and-true choices for impromptu celebrations with friends include the **Old Town Bar** (45 East 18th Street; www.oldtownbar.com) for a classic New York tavern experience.

SPORTS

WATCHING SPORTS

Baseball season is from April through September, and NYC has two major-league teams. The **Mets** play at Citi Field Stadium in Queens (take the 7 subway right to the stadium), and the **Yankees** play in the Bronx (the 4 and D subway lines stop at Yankee Stadium). You can usually buy tickets online at www.mlb.com and sometimes at the stadium on game day.

Football season runs September to January. The **Jets** and the **Giants**, New York City's professional football teams, both play nearby in New Jersey's Meadowlands at MetLife Stadium (there's shuttle-bus service from the Port Authority and a train from Penn Station). Basketball season runs October to April. The **New York Knicks** play at Madison Square Garden at 33rd Street and Seventh Avenue and the Brooklyn Nets play at the Barclay's Center at Atlantic and Flatbush avenues in Brooklyn.

Tickets for football and basketball are hard to come by, but you can try www.stubhub.com, where fans sell tickets they cannot use.

Hockey season generally runs from October to April; the New York team is the **Rangers**, and they play at Madison Square Garden as well. The **US Open Tennis championships** are played at the US Tennis Center in Queens (7 subway to Mets-Willets Point) in late August and early September.

PLAYING SPORTS

Chances are, you didn't come to New York for the great outdoors. But when New Yorkers want to be active they go to **Central Park,** where you can rent a bicycle or a boat (both near the Loeb Boathouse, mid-Park near the Bethesda Terrace), or ice skate in winter (at **Wollman Rink,** mid-Park at 63rd, or **Lasker Rink,** 110th and Lenox Avenue, though the latter is closed until 2024). Otherwise, just follow the example of the many New Yorkers who jog, bike, and skate in Central Park and along the paths that line Hudson River Park. **Bowlero Times Square** (222 West 44th Street; www.bowlero.com) has 48 bowling lanes, games arcade, pool table, and sports bar.

NEW YORK FROM THE WATER

For children and adults, seeing Manhattan from the water is an experience not to be missed. There are great views from the Statue of Liberty and Staten Island ferries (see page 29). In addition, **Circle Line Cruises** (tel: 212-563 3200; www.circleline.com) offers various options, including a 2.5-hour Best of NYC Cruise, the 1.5-hour Landmarks Cruise, and the sunset Harbor Lights Cruise. Cruises leave from Pier 83 at 42nd Street and Twelfth Avenue. On Pier 62 at 22nd Street, Classic Harbor Line (tel: 212-627 1825; www.sail-nyc.com) provides sunset sails aboard their schooners *Adirondack* and America, as well as dinner, jazz, and wine-tasting cruises on their mini-yacht Manhattan.

Chelsea Piers (23rd Street at the Hudson River) is the one all-purpose destination for all your sporting needs. You will find facilities for virtually every sport imaginable, including skating, horseback riding, and swimming. For a complete run-down, tel: 212-336 6666 or www.chelseapiers.com.

Taking 'pictures' of the Statue of Liberty

CHILDREN'S NEW YORK

Central Park offers the greatest number of attractions including the Central Park Zoo and the Carousel. **Madison Square Park** (25th and Madison Avenue) and **Hudson River Park Playground** (Pier 51, Gansevoort Street and Hudson River) are also favourites.

Almost all of New York's museums have exciting offerings for kids; some are devoted entirely to children. At the **Children's Museum of Manhattan** (212 West 83rd Street; www.cmom.org; Mon–Sun 10am–5pm, Sat until 7pm) kids can design their own subway mosaic art, build their own amusement park, or climb a giant Trojan horse while learning about ancient Greece.

For children's theater try the **New Victory Theater** (www.newvictory.org), which makes an effort to present exciting and engaging performances a stone's throw from Times Square.

Many bookstores, including the large chains, have children's story hours. **Books of Wonder** (42 West 17th Street) is the city's oldest and largest independent children's bookstore.

WHAT'S ON

January: Chinese New Year parades and celebrations (Chinatown, Mott, Mulberry and Bayard Streets), late January to mid-February. New York Boat Show.

March: St Patrick's Day Parade (Fifth Avenue) on March 17. Whitney Biennial (in even years, Whitney Museum of American Art).

April: Cherry Blossom Festival (Sakura Matsuri; Brooklyn Botanic Garden), late April–early May. Tribeca Film Festival (various locations), late April.

May: Ninth Avenue International Food Festival (9th Avenue/37th to 57th streets), early to mid-May. Fleet Week, late May.

June: Pride Day Parade (Fifth Avenue & West Village), usually last Sunday in June. Museum Mile Festival (Fifth Avenue/82nd and 105th Streets), usually 2nd Tuesday in June. SummerStage (Central Park), June through September. Midsummer Night's Swing (Lincoln Center), late-June–July. Shakespeare in the Park (The Delacorte Theater in Central Park), June through August.

July: Macy's Fourth of July Fireworks (Hudson River), July 4th.

August: Harlem Week (venues throughout Harlem), throughout August. US Open Tennis Championship (Flushing Meadows, Queens), late August–early September.

September: Feast of San Gennaro (Little Italy), late September. 9/11 Commemorations on September 11. New York Film Festival (Lincoln Center venues), late September to early October.

October: Halloween Parade (Greenwich Village, Sixth Avenue/Spring and 23rd Streets), October 31.

November: New York City Marathon (throughout city), 1st Sunday in November. Macy's Thanksgiving Day Parade (77th Street and Central Park to Broadway and 34th Street), Thanksgiving Day. Radio City Music Hall Christmas Spectacular (Radio City Music Hall), throughout November and December.

December: Christmas Tree Lighting (Rockefeller Center), late November/early December. New Year's Eve (Times Square), December 31.

FOOD AND DRINK

In a city with more than 26,000 restaurants, New Yorkers dine out a lot. You'll find some of the best restaurants in the country in New York, and some are quite expensive, but you won't have to take out a second mortgage on your home to eat well in this city either – even in Manhattan. The variety of restaurants and eating options is unsurpassed. You can enjoy Indian dosas from a street vendor, dine at the latest celebrity chef's restaurant, or simply enjoy a really great meal at a favorite neighborhood spot.

PRICE

You can eat incredibly well in New York for an average amount of money. Dinner (including one drink and tip) generally costs around $50 per person. A good way to experience some of the best (and often most expensive) restaurants, without blowing your budget, is to drop in for lunch instead of dinner. The lunch menu is almost always cheaper. For example, a six-course lunch at Jean-Georges (see page 114) costs $149; a six-course dinner menu starts at $258, even though the quality and variety of the offerings are similar. Prix-fixe meals, particularly pre-theater dinners (usually served 6–7pm) are vastly cheaper than the à la carte menu and are being offered with increasing frequency. If food is the focus of your trip, then plan your visit around one of the seasonal 'NYC Restaurant Weeks,' when more than 380 top-end restaurants offer bargain two-course prix fixe lunches (around $29) and three-course dinners (around $59).

MEALS AND MEAL TIMES

Breakfast is usually served from 7am through at least 9am. Brunch is usually just on weekends, 11am–3pm. Lunch is generally noon–2pm. Dinner is served anywhere from 5.30pm until 11pm, or later in some places. New Yorkers tend to eat dinner a bit later than elsewhere in the US and you will find restaurants busiest between 7pm and 9pm.

NEW YORK SPECIALTIES

Iconic delis and the pastrami sandwich

Pastrami with mustard on rye: the quintessential New York sandwich. Delis all over the United States lay claim to a New York-style pastrami sandwich, but the best are served in authentic New York delicatessens, where you will pay around $15 for a sandwich. Pastrami starts first with beef brisket cured in brine, which is then smoked to give it its unique flavor. It is sliced thick or thin (usually your choice) and served with mustard on rye for a tender and juicy melt-in-your-mouth sandwich.

Early immigrants brought the Eastern European tradition of salted and cured meats to New York. Katz's Delicatessen in the lower East Side opened in 1888 and was immortalized in the famous deli scene in the film *When Harry Met Sally*. During the heyday of New York's leading delis, struggling actors rubbed shoulders at the counters with celebrities, presidents, and New

FOOD HALLS

With the success of Eataly (www.eataly.com/us_en), opened in 2010, and Smorgasburg, the Brooklyn food fair that debuted in 2011, gourmet food halls and markets are now all the rage in New York. Try Mercado Little Spain (www.littlespain.com) in Hudson Yards, Essex Market (www.essexmarket.nyc) in the Lower East Side, Dekalb Market Hall (www.dekalbmarkethall.com) in Brooklyn, Le District (www.ledistrict.com) in the financial district and many more.

York movers and shakers. Those days may have passed, but it's not too late to visit one of these iconic delis: **Barney Greengrass** (541 Amsterdam Avenue; www.barneygreengrass. com); **Carnegie Deli** (Madison Square Garden sections 105/106 and 219, tel: 212-757 2245; www.carnegiedeli.com); **Katz's** (205 East Houston at Ludlow, tel: 212-254 2246; www.katzsdelicatessen.com); and **2nd Ave. Deli** (162 East 33rd Street between Lexington and Third avenues, tel: 212-689 9000; www.2ndavedeli.com).

Diners and coffee shops

You will find diners and coffee shops dotted around every neighborhood of New York, usually with vast menus and reasonable prices. The diner immortalized in the sitcom *Seinfeld* (and in Suzane Vega's 1987 song Tom's Diner) is **Tom's Restaurant** (2880 Broadway at 112th Street; www.tomsrestaurant.net), but it's only the front that you'll recognize.

Bakeries

The city's neighborhoods have some lovely local bakeries. They are great places to pick up a sandwich, breakfast pastry, or sweet cupcake treat. **Dominique Ansel Bakery** (189 Spring Street; www. dominiqueanselny.com), in SoHo, offers tarts, sandwiches, scones, and other treats, but is really famous for having invented the Cronut in 2013 (lines still form to buy them). **Le Pain Quotidien** (locations throughout Manhattan; www.lepainquotidien.com) is a Belgian chain where you can sit at communal tables and enjoy delicious fresh bread, tarts, and pastries. Francophiles should also pay a visit to **Maison Ladurée** (at 864 Madison Ave; www.laduree. fr) famous for its macarons which come in a variety of flavours, such as caramel, framboise, praline and cinnamon-raisin. With its antique upholstered chairs and vintage-style wallpaper, the interior resembles the original 156-year old patisserie.

Bagels

Bagels were allegedly invented in New York, and the best examples can still be found here. Aficionados argue over where to find the perfect bagel, but you won't go wrong with **Ess-a-Bagel** (831 Third Avenue; www.ess-a-bagel.com), **Murray's** (500 Sixth Avenue; www.murraysbagels.com), or one of the many neighborhood bagel shops. All that can be said for certain is that bagels need to be fresh (no more than a few hours old), so stick to the shops that make their own. Add cream cheese, lox (smoked salmon) and a

BRUNCH

If you are in New York over a weekend, then you should try to have Saturday or Sunday brunch. New Yorkers love lazy weekend brunches, which are served at most restaurants, usually starting at 11am (sometimes earlier) through late afternoon (3–4pm). Take the hefty Sunday *New York Times* with you and enjoy. Best to try to go earlier than noon if you don't want to wait. It is normal to see groups of people waiting patiently outside their favorite brunch spots. Diners also provide good brunch options.

squeeze of lemon, and you have a great New York meal.

Pizza

New York is known for pizza, though as anyone who has ever bought a tepid slice from one of the city's pizzerias can tell you, it's not all of the best quality. However, there is infinite variety, from thin crust to thick and chewy to artisanal, oven-baked pizzas. **John's** (278 Bleecker Street; www.johnsofbleecker.com) will never

Queuing for a slice of Grimaldi's pizza

do you wrong, though they don't sell single slices. In Little Italy, the clam pie is popular at **Lombardi's** (32 Spring Street; www.firstpizza.com), the godfather of New York pizza since 1905. **Di Fara Pizza** (1424 Avenue J, Brooklyn; www.difarapizzany.com) in Brooklyn, is generally regarded as the greatest old school pizza joint, with Prince Street Pizza (27 Prince Street; www.princestreetpizzamenu.com) the modern contender in Nolita. Several pizzerias use the name, but there's only one official **Patsy's**, an institution in East Harlem since 1933 (2287 First Avenue, between 117th and 118th streets).

New York cheesecake

This is the classic, New York comfort food, available almost everywhere in many variations. A graham cracker crumb crust is topped with a rich, smooth cheesecake to make a delicious treat. The cheesecake at **Junior's** shouldn't be missed (Times Square, West 45th Street between Broadway and Eighth Avenue, or the original

The original Shake Shack in Madison Square Park

location in Brooklyn, 386 Flatbush Avenue Extension at Dekalb Avenue; www.juniorscheesecake.com).

Steakhouses

Carnivores will delight in the almost 100 steakhouse options in New York. One of the best is **Gallaghers Steakhouse** (228 West 52nd Street; www.gallaghersnysteakhouse.com); **Old Homestead** (56 Ninth Avenue; www.theoldhomesteadsteakhouse.com) is a classic; and **Peter Luger** (178 Broadway at Driggs Street; www.peterluger.com) in Williamsburg, Brooklyn, is often cited as the city's, if not the country's, best place for a porterhouse.

Burgers and hot dogs

The perfect budget meal, the hot dog makes you feel like a real New Yorker, whether you are grabbing one at Yankee Stadium or making a pit stop at a street cart after a night of dancing. The following are all good options: the quirky **Crif Dogs** (113 Saint Marks Place in the East Village; www.crifdogs.com) with its wide range of specialty dogs; the venerable **Papaya King** (179 East 86th Street; www.facebook.com/papayaking); and **Gray's Papaya** (2090 Broadway; https://grayspapaya.nyc). The king of them all is Coney Island's Nathan's Famous (1205 Boardwalk West; www.nathansfamous.com).

New burger joints seem to open all the time. You will find burgers served in restaurants in every price range, from the top restaurants to the popular Shake Shack chain. The following all serve highly rated burgers: the burger joint at **Le Parker Meridien** (119 West 56th Street between Sixth and Seventh avenues; www.burger-jointny.com/56thstreet); **Paul's Da Burger Joint** (131 2nd Avenue; www.paulsburgersnyc.com); Minetta Tavern (113 MacDougal Street; www.minettatavernny.com); **Corner Bistro** (331 West 4th Street at Jane Street; www.cornerbistrony.com); and the **Shake Shack** (original outdoor stand in Madison Square Park, and other locations in Manhattan, Brooklyn, and Queens; www.shakeshack.com).

Carts

Some of the best food in New York is served on sidewalks – and it is not just hot dogs and pretzels. You can find Indian dosas, bratwurst, kebabs, steamed rolled rice noodles, and Mexican tamales. Many of the best vendors are located in the outer boroughs (Queens, in particular), but there is a fair share in Manhattan. Just look for the cart with the line and follow the New Yorkers. Many New Yorkers pick up their breakfast on the street from carts serving coffee, bagels, muffins, and breakfast pastries. A small coffee costs about $1, which is about as cheap as you will get.

Healthy fast food options

The following are all reliable, quick, relatively healthy, and inexpensive options while on the go. **Au Bon Pain** (www.aubonpain.com) is a bakery/café chain serving quality soups, salads, rice and pasta dishes, sandwiches, and pastries at many locations throughout the city. **Hale and Hearty Soups** (several locations in midtown; www.haleandhearty.com) serves soup that is well worth the price. **Whole Foods Market**, with seven locations throughout the city (www.wholefoodsmarket.com) is a chain of natural foods supermarkets with self-serve cafeterias and a wide variety of prepared foods.

ETHNIC ENCLAVES

Chinatown (see page 71) is the best-known locale for Chinese cuisine in New York, but less well publicized is Flushing, Queens, which has a number of excellent Chinese restaurants with some of the best dim sum around. It's also a great spot to try some great Taiwanese or Malaysian food. You will find a group of Vietnamese restaurants on Baxter Street, Chinatown, not far from the US Courthouse.

Dumplings and wonton soup in Chinatown

Though **Little Italy** has shrunk to a couple of blocks of Mulberry Street north of Canal Street, there are still Italian restaurants that can pass muster; most of the places here will do if all you want is a plate of pasta and a glass of wine. Another group of Italian restaurants can be found on Bleecker Street between Thompson Street and Seventh Avenue.

Curry Row on Sixth Street between First and Second avenues, has some very cheap Indian restaurants, only a handful of which are actually good (Panna II at 93 First Avenue, is one of the best; www.pannatwo.com).

The above are some of the most popular options, but you can find food from almost anywhere in the world: Brazilian restaurants can be found in a cluster on 45th and 46th streets in Midtown (between Sixth and Seventh avenues), and Korean eateries dot 32nd Street between Fifth Avenue and Broadway, while Egyptian places are concentrated over in Long Island City. For a multi-ethnic feast, investigate Ninth Avenue in the 40s and 50s.

WHERE TO EAT

We have used the following symbols to give an idea of the average price for a three-course meal for one, not including drinks or tip:

$$$$	$50–100
$$$	$35–50
$$	$25–35
$	below $25

DOWNTOWN

Cafeteria $$ *119 7th Avenue (at 17th), tel: 212-414 1717;* www.cafeteriagroup. com. One of Chelsea's trendy options, Cafeteria is open 24 hours and offers reconstructed bistro and diner food for hip club-goers. Where else will you be able to get pancakes or grilled salmon at 4.30am? Consistently good, if not overly exciting.

Eataly $$$ *200 5th Avenue (at 23rd), tel: 212-229 2560;* www.eataly.com. The brainchild of the Bastianich family, this market and gourmet food court is always swarmed with folks sampling the imported Italian fare, from pizza, panini, and pasta, to espresso, beer and gelato. There are sit-down restaurants, bars and takeout stands; something for every taste and budget.

Eleven Madison Park $$$$ *11 Madison Avenue (at 24th), tel: 212-889 0905;* www.elevenmadisonpark.com. This restaurant keeps getting better and better. One of the most elegant dining rooms in the city, with ceilings that reach into the clouds, this Flatiron business lunch staple is also one of the best places for dinner, garnering three Michelin stars.

Gotham Bar and Grill $$$$ *12 East 12th Street (5th Avenue and University), tel: 212-620 4020;* www.gothambarandgrill.com. This large, airy space is usually filled with well-dressed downtowners who appreciate the exquisite food and well-chosen, but expensive wines. Few other upscale restaurants are as inviting to single diners, who can order and eat at the bar in comfort and style. The fixed-price restaurant week lunch is a great deal.

Gramercy Tavern $$$$ *42 E. 20th Street (between Broadway & Park), tel: 212-477 0777; www.gramercytavern.com.* Seasonally inspired fresh and local ingredients are the focus of this popular New American tavern with excellent service. Reservations are often difficult to come by, but you can also eat in the front tavern, which accepts walk-ins. Tasting menus available for lunch and dinner.

Hangawi $$$ *12 East 32nd Street (5th and Madison avenues), tel: 212-213 0077; www.hangawirestaurant.com.* Diners at this vegetarian Korean restaurant will quickly become suffused with a Zen-like calm. Discard your cares (and your shoes) at the door, and try mountain-root vegetables, porridges, and other delicacies.

Hill Country $$ *30 West 26th Street (at Broadway), tel: 212-255 4544; www. hillcountry.com/nyc.* This Texas barbecue near the Empire State Building is justly celebrated for its brisket, sausage and honky-tonk atmosphere. It is more expensive than a roadside stand, but from Tuesday through Saturday there are live music shows, most free to the public.

Il Buco $$$$ *47 Bond Street, tel: 212-533 1932; www.ilbuco.com.* An intimate place to sample hearty Italian and Mediterranean fare, this former antique shop fills up with couples and small parties who appreciate the rustic preparations of meat and pasta, the excellent wine list, and the cluttered, but cozy setting.

Ivan Ramen $$ *25 Clinton St, between Stanton and Houston sts, tel: 646-678 3859; www.ivanramen.com.* Chef Ivan Orkin (who also runs restaurants in Tokyo) helms this popular ramen noodle joint adorned with a huge papier-mâché mural. Menu highlights include the sesame noodles, the spicy red chilli ramen and the steamed pork buns.

Kanoyama $$$$ *175 2nd Avenue (at 11th), tel: 212-777 5266; www.kanoyama.com.* East Village Japanese restaurant with a strong following. The portions are generous and the fish is incredibly fresh. Friendly staff.

Momofuku Noodle Bar $$ *171 1st Avenue, tel: 212- 777 7773; www.momofukunoodlebar.com.* An eccentric masterpiece and part of David Chang's ever-expanding Momofuku empire. What started as a 'Korean burrito bar' has become one of the city's hippest and tables, serving innovative cuisine inspired by Korea, the American South, and everywhere in between. Favorites include the pork belly buns, the smoked chicken wings and various bowls of aromatic ramen; smoked pork, ginger scallion, chilled spicy, garlic chicken and more. Other Momofuku restaurants are all worth a visit, including Bang Bar, Milk Bar, and tiny, but wondrous Ko.

Nobu Downtown $$$$ *195 Broadway, tel: 212-219 0500;* www.noburestaurants.com. Still wildly popular and trendy (forget Saturday night), Nobu continues to pack in crowds with its innovative nouvelle Japanese menu. There is another Nobu restaurant at 40 West 57th Street (tel: 212-757 3000).

Noodle Village $ *13 Mott Street (near Chatham Square), tel: 212-233 0788.* This Cantonese restaurant at the southern end of Mott Street in Chinatown boasts that their chef arrived straight from Hong Kong. They also proudly claim that there is no MSG added to their dishes. The congee and noodle soups are popular choices. A great cheap, healthy and fast option.

Nyonya $ *199 Grand Street (at Mulberry), tel: 212-334 3669;* www.ilovenyonya.com. This is the place to go for an introduction to the delicious and spicy cuisine of Malaysia. The Hainanese chicken is good, but don't overlook spicy beef rendang or one of the equally tasty seafood dishes.

Russ & Daughters Café $$$ *127 Orchard St, between Delancey and Rivington streets), tel: 212-475 4880;* https://russanddaughters.com. The original Manhattan gourmet shop (set up in 1914 to sate the appetites of homesick immigrant Jews) opened this excellent café in 2014, serving amazing hand-rolled bagels, knishes, pickled herring and classics like sturgeon, eggs and onions.

Shabu-Tatsu $$ *216 East 10th Street (between 1st and 2nd avenues), tel: 212-477 2972;* www.shabutatsu.com. At this small, popular Japanese restaurant, diners choose a selection of thinly sliced meats and vegetables for *shabu-shabu* (swirled in a hot pot of seasoned water), sukiyaki (a Japanese stew), or yakiniku (cooked on a grill) and cook it themselves in the middle of the table.

Tamarind Tribeca $$$$ *99 Hudson Street (at Franklin Street), tel: 212-775 9000;* www.tamarindtribeca.com. There are plenty of mediocre Indian restaurants in the city, but this is an innovative and elegant take on the cuisine, leaps beyond the typical samosas and chicken tikka masala. The excellent four-course lunch is $32.

Union Square Café $$$$ *101 East 19th Street, tel: 212-243 4020;* www.union-squarecafe.com. Gracious service and reliably good food are two reasons why this restaurant remains one of New York's perennial favorites. Although the Mediterranean-inspired cuisine is no longer cutting-edge, the food still dazzles in unexpected ways. Even the fried calamari, now a restaurant staple, is heads above the chewy appetizer most people have come to expect. The extensive and reasonably priced wine list is an added bonus.

Veselka $$ *144 Second Ave (at 9th), tel: 212-228 9682;* www.veselka.com. This always-crowded 24hr Ukrainian diner ("Veselka" means "rainbow" in Ukrainian) has been an East Village institution since 1954, offering fine home-made hot borscht (and cold in summer), locally-made kielbasa sausage, veal goulash and pierogi. It also serves excellent bagels with cream cheese (you can order to go).

MIDTOWN

Aquavit $$$$ *65 East 55th Street (at Madison and Park avenues), tel: 212-307 7311;* www.aquavit.org. Like the Scandinavian fare served here, the décor is modern, precise and minimally adorned. There is fish on the menu, of course, but also meatballs, squab and beef. Try a glass of the eponymous spirits.

Becco $$$ *355 West 46th Street (8th and 9th avenues), tel: 212-397 7597;* www.becco-nyc.com. Come for the delicious pasta at this rustic Theater District favorite, which combines reasonable prices and high quality. The two-course fixed-price meal is particularly good value, especially since the pasta is an all-you-can-eat special.

Le Bernardin $$$$ *155 West 51st Street, tel: 212-554 1515;* www.le-bernardin.com. Eric Ripert has carved out his niche, and no one is complaining. Le Bernardin serves only seafood and only the city's best. Every item on the fixed-price menu is a winner, from the simplest pan-seared cod to a whole-roasted red snapper for two. Divinely inspired desserts. No lunch Sat. Closed Sun.

La Bonne Soupe $$ *48 West 55st Street, tel: 212-586 7650; www.labonnenyc. com.* The line is always long at this reliable French bistro around the corner from MoMA, where they have been dishing out steak frites, quiche, omelettes, fondues, and excellent onion soup for 40 years.

Carmine's $$$ *200 West 44th Street (Broadway and 8th Avenue), tel: 212-221 3800; www.carminesnyc.com.* The huge portions of hearty Italian food at this Theater District mainstay are served family-style, so the prices aren't as high as they seem at first glance. Always mobbed and loud, but consistently churning out massive quantities of food at all hours, this is a reliable standby eatery.

Charlie Palmer Steak NYC $$$$ *One Bryant Park, 135 West 42nd Street (at Broadway and 6th Avenue), tel: 212-319 1660; www.charliepalmersteak.com.* This is arguably the best steakhouse in the Times Square neighborhood. It is certainly one of the most expensive, but the pre-theater prix-fixe menu, and the happy hour (Tue–Fri 4–6pm) are great deals.

Churrascaria Plataforma $$$ *316 West 49th Street (8th and 9th avenues), tel: 212-245 0505; www.plataformaonline.com.* All-you-can eat Brazilian rodízios (huge meat-heavy buffet) make this one of the most popular and fun places to go when you are in the mood to eat, and eat a lot. Start at the salad bar, a healthy prelude to the parade of skewered meats, which doesn't stop until you're about to explode. A *caipirinha* cocktail will set your taste buds on the right track.

DB Bistro Moderne $$$$ *55 West 44th Street (between 5th and 6th avenues), tel: 212-391 2400; www.dbbistro.com.* Chef Daniel Boulud's bistro is awash in culinary surprises and Art Deco glitz, with a clientele to match. The burger is a modern classic, made with sirloin, short ribs, foie gras and black truffles.

The Grill $$$$ *99 East 52nd Street (between Lexington and Park avenues), tel: 212-375 9001; https://thegrillnewyork.com.* Located in the Seagram Building, chef Mario Carbone creates impeccable American specialties in this mid-century style chophouse. Prime aged steaks, including the classic porterhouse, lobster and duck are included in the variety of seafood and meat dishes available. Cocktails also remain classic with the Manhattan, champagne cocktail and a variety of martinis on the menu. Lunch Tue–Fri only, closed Sun and Mon.

Russian Tea Room $$$$ *150 West 57th St (between 6th and 7th avenues), tel: 212-581 7100;* www.russiantearoomnyc.com. Founded by members of the Russian Imperial Ballet in 1927, Madonna once worked the coat check at this iconic restaurant. In its third incarnation, with whimsical, modernist Russian-style décor, it has nowhere near the cachet of the original, but it still pulls folks in – the stroganoff and the chicken Kiev are faves.

Sardi's $$$ *234 West 44th Street at Broadway and Eighth Ave, tel: 212-221 8440;* www.sardis.com. Of course, lunch and dinner are served at this legendary Theater District mainstay, but even if you're not drinking, a drink at the bar is a must. Sip a cocktail surrounded by the trademark caricatures of every Broadway name. Friendly barmen.

Smith and Wollensky $$$$ *49th Street (at 3rd Avenue), tel: 212-753 1530;* www.smithandwollensky.com. The well-aged steaks served in this classic restaurant are consistently and perfectly grilled. The wine list is excellent, although expensive; sometimes shockingly so. The less expensive grill just around the corner is a good alternative for anyone without an expense account.

THE UPPER EAST SIDE

Café Sabarsky $$$ *1048 5th Avenue (at 86th Street), tel: 212-288 0665;* www.neuegalerie.org/cafesabarsky. Enter this wood-paneled salon within the Neue Galerie (see page 53), and you'll think you're on Vienna's Ringstrasse. Executive Chef Christopher Engel lives up to the surroundings, while museum food is taken to new heights by the beef goulash, Viennese sausage, linzer torte, and other fare from the banks of the Danube.

Daniel $$$$ *60 East 65th Street (near Park Avenue), tel: 212-288 0033;* www.danielnyc.com. Daniel Boulud has mastered the art of casual elegance. His flagship restaurant in New York is still the best, a pricey but delectable treat, with refined French techniques blended with local seafood, vegetables and meats. The four-course seasonal prix fixe menu is the way to go.

The Loeb Boathouse $$$$ *Central Park, enter on East 72nd Street, tel: 212-517 2233;* www.thecentralparkboathouse.com. The lake and surrounding greenery of Central Park are the most memorable part of a meal in this airy, glass-fronted dining room and waterside terrace (the perfect spot for a warm-weather brunch). True to the watery surroundings, the kitchen sends out such nautically inspired flourishes as sea urchin and caviar in a scallop shell and pan-roasted monkfish and seared wild striped sea bass. Meanwhile, brunchtime hits of the French toast and omelette variety satisfy the hungry weekend crowds.

Pastrami Queen $$ *1125 Lexington Avenue (at East 78th Street), tel: 212-734 1500; www.pastramiqueen.com.* This friendly diner has been knocking out giant hot pastrami sandwiches since 1956, as well as corned beef and a host of Jewish kosher classics (such as matzoh-ball soups, knish, stuffed cabbage and kreplach, Jewish dumplings) and desserts. There is a second location on the Upper West Side at 138 West 72nd Street.

Sfoglia $$$$ *1402 Lexington Avenue (at 92nd Street), tel: 212-831 1402; www. sfogliarestaurant.com.* This New York branch of the original Nantucket restaurant is just as at home on the Upper East Side. An unobtrusive little trattoria, it offers seasonal Northern Italian country fare in a casual and intimate setting. Diners return for the inventive, frequently changing menu. There are only ten tables, so plan ahead for dinner reservations. The homemade bread is to die for.

The View $$$$ *1535 Broadway (at 45th and 46th streets), tel: 212-704 8900; www.theviewnyc.com.* High atop the Marriott Marquis Hotel in Times Square is New York's only revolving restaurant, with a wonderful panoramic view of the skyline.

THE UPPER WEST SIDE

Awash Ethiopian Restaurant $$$ *947 Amsterdam Ave, between 106th and 107th streets, tel: 212-961 1416; www.awashny.com.* Ethiopian expats flock to this brightly coloured restaurant offering sumptuous vegetarian and meat combo platters. Dig in with your hands, but lay off the too-sweet honey wine. There are also convenient branches in the East Village and in Brooklyn.

Barney Greengrass $$ *541 Amsterdam Avenue (between 86th and 87th streets), tel: 212-724 4707; www.barneygreengrass.com.* The faded murals and formica tables are deceptively downbeat, but New Yorkers continue to herald this West Side institution as the best place in town for lox, smoked sturgeon, chopped liver, and other Jewish fare. Weekend lines are long, but in them you might spot Bill Murray, Woody Allen, and other celebrity regulars. Closed Monday.

Jacob's Pickles $$$ *509 Amsterdam Ave, at 85th Street, tel: 212-470 5566;* http://jacobs.picklehospitality.com. Southern fare like stacks of pancakes teetering with fried chicken, biscuits slathered in mushroom gravy, mac and cheese and (of course) superbly tart and tangy pickles. Everything is served up in a fun, noisy, modern dining room with exposed brick and long leather banquettes.

Jean-Georges $$$$ *1 Central Park West (at 60th and 61st streets, in the Trump International Hotel), tel: 212-299 3900;* www.jean-georges.com. Chef Jean-Georges Vongerichten's four-star experiment in ultra-chic surroundings is well worth the price. For the ultimate, try the seasonally focused tasting menu; for the experience of just being here, order the prix-fixe lunch at a fraction of the cost.

Sarabeth's $$$ *423 Amsterdam Avenue (between 80th and 81st streets), tel: 212-496 6280;* www.sarabethsrestaurants.com. Cheery and incredibly popular, Sarabeth's is best for its home-style breakfasts and brunch, from waffles to fluffy eggs, although succulent roasts and other serious and well-prepared dishes come out at dinnertime. Child-friendly environs and homey decor. There are three other locations: at 339 Greenwich Street, corner of Jay Street, tel: 212-966 0421; at 381 Park Avenue South, between 26th and 27th streets, tel: 212-335 0093; and at 40 Central Park South, tel: 212-826 5959.

Shun Lee West $$$$ *43 West 65th Street (Columbus Avenue and Central Park West), tel: 212-595 8895;* www.shunleerestaurants.com. Those used to take-out noodles, fried rice, and General Tso's chicken will be amazed at how refined Chinese food can be. Serving up traditional Cantonese, Szechuan and Hunan specialities. Attached to the original restaurant is the much less expensive Shun Lee Café serving up steamed and fried dim sum.

Tessa $$$ *349 Amsterdam Avenue, tel: 212-390 1974;* www.tessarestaurant.com. A popular Mediterranean tavern combining French, Italian and Spanish cuisines, located close to Central Park and the Beacon Theater. Chef Nicholas McCann produces dishes based on locally sourced, fresh, produce as well as speciality ingredients thus, the extensive menu changes seasonally. There is an extensive wine list to choose from offering wines from around the globe.

TRAVEL ESSENTIALS

PRACTICAL INFORMATION

A Accommodations 116

Airports 116

B Bicycle Rental 118

Budgeting for
your trip 118

C Car rental/hire 119

Climate 119

Clothing 120

Crime and safety 120

Customs regulations 121

D Driving 121

E Electricity 122

Embassies and
consulates 122

Emergencies 123

G Getting there 123

Guides and tours 123

H Health and
medical care 124

L LGBTQ+ travelers 125

Lost property 125

M Maps 125

Media 125

Money 126

O Opening hours 126

P Police 127

Post offices 127

Public holidays 127

T Telephones 127

Time zones 128

Tipping 128

Toilets 129

Tourist information 129

Transportation 129

Travelers with
disabilities 131

V Visas and entry
requirements 131

W Websites 131

Weights and
measures 131

Y Youth hostels and
YMCAs 131

A

ACCOMMODATION (See also Youth hostels and YMCAs and the list of Recommended hotels)

It is increasingly hard to find a decent yet reasonably priced hotel room in New York. Despite a dip during the Covid-19 pandemic, the average price of a hotel room in Manhattan is still about $250 per night. The high season is fall and winter, particularly from late November through New Year's Day, when rates can be as much as 25 percent higher; the low season is January through mid-March, though some hotels also reduce rates in the summer. Advance reservations are often crucial; the city is very crowded. Be aware that quoted rates will not include a sales tax of 14.75 percent, plus a $3.50 per day occupancy tax. Most hotels do not provide breakfast. At many hotels children can sleep in their parents' room at no extra charge.

Bed and breakfasts have largely disappeared from Manhattan, though you'll find some in Harlem and the Outer Boroughs. Good websites to search include www.bnbfinder.com. Apartment rentals through websites such as Airbnb (www.airbnb.com) and Vrbo (www.vrbo.com) are an increasingly popular alternative in the city, though legally, these must be rooms in a home that permanent residents are living in (otherwise you can only legally rent apartments on these websites for stays of over 30 days). It is a good option if you want to feel part of the city and at home in a neighbourhood, from brownstones in Park Slope to tiny hip apartments in Williamsburg or the East Village.

AIRPORTS

New York is served by three major airports: **John F. Kennedy International** (JFK) and **Newark Liberty International** (EWR), the two international airports, and **LaGuardia** (LGA), mostly for domestic flights.

John F. Kennedy Airport (tel: 718-244 4444; www.jfkairport.com) is in Queens, about 15 miles (24km) southeast of midtown Manhattan. The JFK AirTrain (www.jfkairport.com/to-from-airport/air-train), combined with the subway (or Long Island Rail Road), is the cheapest way to get into town, but the total journey time into Manhattan usually takes well over an hour. The AirTrain operates 24 hours a day, every 7 to 12 minutes during peak times (4–7.30am and 3–8pm) and every 15 or 20 minutes during non-peak hours, from all terminals. Take the AirTrain (www.new.mta.info/guides/airports; $8) to Howard Beach where you can connect with the A subway train ($2.75), or to Jamaica station for the E, J, or Z subway trains ($2.75), or the faster Long Island Rail Road (LIRR) to Penn Station ($5.25–17). A taxi from the airport to any destination below 96th Street in Manhattan takes about 45 minutes to an hour, depending on traffic, and costs $52 flat rate, not including tolls, peak hours surcharge ($4.50, 4-8pm Mon–Fri) or tip. Rides to Brooklyn ($52–55) and the other boroughs are on the meter. Shuttle buses cost around $20–25 per person: try ETS Airport Shuttle (www.etsairportshuttle.com), Go Airlink (www.goairlinkshuttle.com), or SuperShuttle (www.supershuttle.com).

Newark Liberty Airport (tel: 973-961 6000; www.newarkairport.com) is located in New Jersey, 16 miles (26km) southwest of midtown Manhattan. Newark is usually more convenient than JFK for those staying in the Theater District. Taxis to Midtown take 30–45 minutes and metered fares usually run around $55–80, not including additions for tolls for the tunnels (at least $13 extra) and tip. Newark Airport Express (www.coachusa.com/airport-transportation/newark-airport) shuttle costs about $17 (one way) per person to Grand Central Terminal, the Port Authority Bus Terminal on 42nd Street, or Bryant Park. AirTrain Newark (www.newarkairport.com/to-from-airport/air-train) takes you from all terminals to Newark Liberty station, where you can take a NJ Transit (www.njtransit.com) commuter train to Penn Station in around 30 minutes (note these can be busy and are not equipped to handle large pieces of luggage). The AirTrain operates every 3 minutes during peak times (5am–midnight), every 10 minutes during non-peak hours, 24 hours a day; NJ Transit commuter train schedules vary (6am–midnight). The total cost is about $15.25 (the $7.75 AirTrain ticket is included when you buy your NJ Transit ticket).

LaGuardia Airport (tel: 718-533 3400; www.laguardiaairport.com) is located in Queens, 8 miles (13km) northeast of midtown Manhattan. Taxis to Midtown take 30–40 minutes depending on traffic and usually cost $35–$45, not including tolls or tip. The trip by subway and bus can take considerably longer than a taxi but costs only $2.75 if you purchase a MetroCard. The M60 SBS bus connects with the subways in northern Manhattan; Q70 SBS, Q47, Q72 and Q48 buses connect with the subway in Queens.

B

BICYCLE RENTAL

Cycling is becoming a viable form of transport around New York, most enjoyable if you stick to the city's two hundred miles of bike lanes (www.nycbike-maps.com) as well as the cycle paths along the waterfront and in parks. Wear all possible safety equipment including pads and a helmet (required by law). When you park, double-chain and lock your bike (including wheels) to an immovable object if you'd like it to be there when you return.

In 2013, New York started a bike share scheme dubbed Citi Bike (www.citi-bikenyc.com), with thousands of bikes and hundreds of stations all over the city. There are three payment options: Day Pass ($15; unlimited 30min rides within 24hrs), Single Ride ($3.99 for 30min), or annual membership ($185; unlimited 45min rides). Pay at any Citi Bike station kiosk with a credit card.

Traditional bike rentals start at about $15–16 per hour or $45–55 per day – which means opening to closing (9.30am–6.30pm for instance). Try Bike Rent (www.bikerent.nyc) or Unlimited Biking (www.unlimitedbiking.com/new-york).

BUDGETING FOR YOUR TRIP

Flights to New York: Airfares to New York depend on the season and can fluctuate wildly. The highest prices are generally between May and September; you'll get the best prices by booking months in advance or flying during the low season, November to February (excluding late Nov until early Jan, the holiday season).

Hotel: For a double room (before tax), expect to pay over $150 per night for a budget room, up to $275 for a moderate room, up to $350 for an expensive room, and over $500 for a luxury room. The only way to spend less than $100 per night is to stay in a hostel or YMCA.

Meals: Breakfast can be had for $6–8; lunch costs from $8–10 for a sandwich and drink from a deli to $12–15 in an inexpensive restaurant; dinner can cost anywhere from $20 to over $200 per person. A glass of wine is rarely less than $8, and a bottle is considered very cheap at $25.

Transportation: An unlimited MetroCard for one week costs $33.

Museums and attractions: Some museums and attractions are expensive ($25 each for the Guggenheim, Met and MoMA), but many museums are free at least one evening a week.

C

CAR RENTAL/HIRE (See also Driving)

We don't recommend that you rent a car unless you plan to leave the city proper, since New York City has the highest car rental and parking rates in the US (as much as $80 per day). If you do need a car, though, you will find that it's generally cheaper to rent one at the airport than in Manhattan, and it's cheaper still to rent a car outside of New York City, where prices are more competitive. We strongly recommend that you make your reservation for car rental before you leave home.

You will need a major credit card to rent a car. The minimum age for renting a car is 21, but some companies will not rent to drivers under-25, or when they do will impose a high additional fee. Rental from JFK is approximately $60–$100/day. You will probably end up paying more in parking fees than rental costs.

Avis (www.avis.com) 800-633 3469
Budget (www.budget.com) 800-218 7992
Enterprise (www.enterprise.com) 844-362 0812
Hertz (www.hertz.com) 800-654 3131

CLIMATE

New York is a city of extremes when it comes to weather. Summers (mid-June to early September) in New York are hot and humid; winters (mid-November to late March) are generally cold. Spring (early April to mid-June) and fall (mid-September to mid-November) have the best weather. While the average low temperature in January is around -2°C, it can be as low as -15°C. The wind is a major factor in how cold it feels when you are walking in the city. In summer it can get very humid with extremes at close to 38°C.

Average temperatures and rainfall in New York City

Jan	Feb	Mar	Apr	May	Jun	Jul	Aug	Sep	Oct	Nov	Dec
Fahrenheit (°F) Max/min temp											
40	42	51	61	71	79	84	82	75	65	54	45
29	30	37	46	56	65	71	69	62	52	42	34
Celsius (°C) Max/min temp											
4	6	10	16	22	26	29	28	24	18	12	7
-2	-1	3	8	13	18	21	21	17	11	6	1
Days of rain/snow											
7	7	8	9	10	10	10	10	8	7	8	8

CLOTHING

Casual dress is fine for most places in New York, including restaurants and theaters. Only a very few restaurants strictly enforce jacket and tie policies. In the summer, light clothing made of natural fibers is recommended because of the heat and humidity. In winter, hats and gloves will go a long way to keeping the wind and cold at bay. Make sure to bring layers to cope with both the very cold and more moderate days.

CRIME AND SAFETY (See also Emergencies)

While New York is the safest major city in the US, petty theft is still common, especially pick-pocketing at crowded intersections and subway train entrances. Most areas of Manhattan and Brooklyn are relatively safe, though the usual precautions should be taken at night. Areas such as Brownsville or East New York in Brooklyn remain sketchy, but you are highly unlikely to end up in either place. If you are robbed, report it to the police (tel: 646-610 5000 or 311 for non-emergencies; 911 for emergencies): your insurance company will need to see a copy of the police report (as may your consulate if your passport is stolen).

CUSTOMS REGULATIONS

You can bring into the US the following duty-free items: one liter of alcohol, if over 21 years of age; 200 cigarettes, 50 cigars, or 2kg of tobacco, if you are over 18; and gifts worth up to $100 ($800 for US citizens. Travelers with more than $10,000 in US or foreign currency, traveler's checks, or money orders must declare these upon entry. Meats, fruits, vegetables, seeds, or plants (and, note, even sealed prepared foods from them) are not permitted and must be disposed in the receptacles provided before entering. For more information, contact US Customs and Border Protection (tel: 877-227 5511; "Know Before You Go" document on www.cbp.gov).

D

DRIVING (See also Car rental/hire)

Driving conditions. Visitors arriving by car would do well to leave their vehicle parked in a garage and use public transportation, as traffic and scarce parking space make driving a nightmare. If you must drive, remember the following rules: the speed limit is 25mph (40kmh) unless otherwise indicated; you may not (legally) use your horn in the city; the use of seat belts is mandatory; the speed limit on most highways in the city is 55mph (90kmh) and strictly enforced – look for signs, as on some major highways it has been raised to 65mph (105kmh); right-hand turns are prohibited at all red lights in the city; and, of course, visitors must remember to drive on the right. Before leaving home, determine whether your own insurance will cover you when you are driving a rented car.

Parking. While street parking is possible in some areas outside of Midtown, a garage or parking lot is the safer though far more expensive choice (www.

bestparking.com/new-york-ny-parking and www.iconparkingsystems.com are useful for locating parking garages at discounted rates). If you find a parking spot, obey parking regulations, which may include parking only on one side of the street on alternate days (call 311 for more information). Never park next to a fire hydrant and don't leave your car over the time limit, or it may be towed away.

Gas (petrol). Service stations are scarce in the city (Eleventh and Twelfth avenues on the West Side are good hunting grounds).

Breakdowns and insurance. AAA Northeast (www.northeast.aaa.com), a branch of the American Automobile Association (AAA), will help members as well as foreign visitors affiliated with other recognized automobile associations. In case of a breakdown call their Emergency Road Service (tel: 800-222 4357) or wait until a police car comes along.

AAA Manhattan: 1881 Broadway, NY 10023, tel: 212-586 1723; www.northeast.aaa.com.

E

ELECTRICITY

110-volt 60-cycle AC is standard throughout the US. Plugs are the flat, parallel two-pronged variety. Foreign visitors without dual-voltage appliances will need a transformer and adapter plug.

EMBASSIES AND CONSULATES

Embassies are located in Washington, DC, but most countries have consulates or missions to the United Nations in New York.

Australia: Consulate General, 150 East 42nd Street, tel: 212-351 6500; www.usa.embassy.gov.au/new-york

Canada: 466 Lexington Avenue, 20th Floor, tel: 1-844-880 6519; www.international.gc.ca

Ireland: 345 Park Avenue, tel: 212-319 2555; www.dfa.ie/irish-consulate/newyork

New Zealand: 295 Madison Avenue, tel: 212-832 4038; www.mfat.govt.nz

South Africa: 845 Third Avenue, 9th and 10th Floors, tel: 917-200 8396; www.southafrica-usa.net/consulate

UK: 1 Dag Hammarskjold Plaza, 885 Second Avenue, tel: 212-745 0200; www.gov.uk/government/world/organisations/british-consulate-general-new-york

EMERGENCIES (See also Health and medical care and Police)

All-purpose emergency number: 911

G

GETTING THERE

By air. Most airlines have several flights a day to one of New York's airports. Newark is a hub for United Airlines (www.united.com); from Europe it is also served by Aer Lingus (Dublin), British Airways (London-Heathrow), low-cost carrier French Bee (Paris), Lufthansa (Frankfurt, Munich), Scandinavian Airlines (Copenhagen, Oslo, Stockholm–Arlanda), Swiss Airlines (Zurich) and TAP Air Portugal (Lisbon); and from Canada by Air Canada (www.aircanada.com).

JFK is a hub for American (www.aa.com), Delta (www.delta.com) and Jet-Blue (www.jetblue.com); connections to most European cities are good, as are connections to Canada, and to Asia and the Pacific via Air China, Cathay Pacific, Emirates, Korean Air and many others. LaGuardia, which serves mostly domestic flights, is a hub of Delta and American; Frontier, JetBlue, Southwest Airlines, Spirit Airlines and United also use LaGuardia, as does Air Canada and WestJet (Calgary).

H

HEALTH AND MEDICAL CARE

New York has many of the country's top hospitals. Payment for any medical services will be billed in full, and the bill will probably be exorbitantly high. Arrange for health insurance before your visit. In an emergency, your hotel should be able to provide a list of doctors. Tap water is perfectly safe in New York.

The Covid-19 pandemic caused major disruption and claimed the lives of over 68,000 New Yorkers as of May 2022. For ongoing restrictions, visitors to New York should check the most up-to-date guidance at https://coronavirus. health.ny.gov/home.

Pharmacies. There are many pharmacies in New York that are open 24 hours including the following:

CVS, 150 East 42nd Street, tel: 212-661 8139; www.cvs.com

CVS, 630 Lexington Avenue at 53rd Street, tel: 917-369 8688

Walgreen's, 1 Union Square South (at 14th Street), tel: 212-677 0214; www. walgreens.com

L

LGBTQ+ TRAVELERS

New York has a sizable LGBTQ+ population. While Greenwich Village, especially Christopher Street, is still a center for gay life, Chelsea is now the more fashionable gay neighborhood, where many gay restaurants and shops can be found (especially along Eighth Avenue from 14th to 23rd streets). For LGBTQ+ events and nightlife information, see *The Village Voice* (www.villagevoice.com) or www.nycgo.com/maps-guides/gay. Publications include *Gay City News* (www.gaycitynews.com), covering local, national and international news. Gay and Lesbian Hotline tel: 212-989 0999. Lesbian, Gay, Bisexual and Transgender Community Center tel: 212-620 7310; https:// gaycenter.org.

LOST PROPERTY

Each transport system maintains its own lost property office. Here are two useful numbers: **New York City Transit Authority** (subway network and bus system) Lost Property Office: tel: 511; www.new.mta.info/lost-and-found/ subway-bus-and-staten-island-railway; and NYC **Taxi and Limousine Commission Lost Property:** tel: 311.

M

MAPS

Most hotels offer free maps but you can also pick them up at Official NYC Information centers and kiosks.

MEDIA

Magazines and newspapers. The city's major daily newspapers are the *Daily News, New York Times,* and *New York Post.* Several local weeklies, including *The New Yorker* and *New York Magazine* have information about goings on about town. *The Village Voice*, also weekly, is an online only publication (www.villagevoice.com).

Radio and television. Channel 1 (NY1) on Spectrum cable systems is a 24-hour station devoted to local news, weather, and events. There are about 50 local AM and FM radio stations in the New York area, including 1010 WINS (AM) for traffic, news, and weather.

MONEY

Currency. There are 100 cents in the dollar. The coins are: 1¢ (penny), 5¢ (nickel), 10¢ (dime), 25¢ (quarter), and $1. Bank notes of $1, $5, $10, $20, $50, and $100 are common, but some places will not accept denominations over $20 unless you make a large purchase.

Exchange. Other than exchange booths at the airport, it's no longer easy to change foreign money into dollars in the city itself. Branches of the Chase Manhattan Bank, Citibank, and the bigger offices of other major banks may change foreign currency, but usually only for account holders. Your best bet is to exchange money at People's Foreign Exchange (24 West 45th Street; www.peoplesfx.com), which is usually open weekdays only 9am–6pm, or at a branch of Currency Exchange International (www.ceifx.com), which has a location at Penn Station (345 7th Avenue).

ATMs. Most banks charge a small fee ($3) to non-depositors to use their ATM machines, but this is usually the most efficient way to get US dollars.

O

OPENING HOURS

Banks: Mon–Fri 9am–3 or 4pm; many open Sat 9am–2pm. Some banks, such as TD Bank, are now offering longer opening hours (7.30am–8pm) and Sunday openings (11am–4pm).

Offices: 9am–5pm is the norm.

Stores: Mon–Sat 10am–6pm; some open until 7 or 8pm and most on Sun noon–6pm.

Restaurants: Most are open until at least 11pm during the week, and until midnight or later on Friday and Saturday. Some are closed on Mondays.

P

POLICE (See also Crime and Emergencies)

In an emergency, dial 911. The New York Police Department (NYPD; www. nypdonline.org) is divided into precincts that cover specific areas; check the website or ask your hotel if you need to visit your local station.

POST OFFICES

Post offices are generally open weekdays 8am–5pm and on Saturday 9am–1pm. New York's General Post Office (421 Eighth Avenue, New York, NY 10001; www.usps.com) has extended hours (Mon–Fri 7am–10pm, Sat 9am–9pm, Sun 11am–7pm). You can buy stamps at hotel reception desks, in many grocery stores, or from stamp machines. Mailboxes are painted blue.

PUBLIC HOLIDAYS

The following are national holidays in the US. In New York City, banks, offices, and some stores and museums are closed on these days:

New Year's Day January 1
Martin Luther King, Jr. Day Third Monday in January
President's Day Third Monday in February

Memorial Day Last Monday in May
Independence Day July 4
Labor Day First Monday in September
Columbus Day Second Monday in October
Veterans' Day November 11
Thanksgiving Day Fourth Thursday in November
Christmas Day December 25

T

TELEPHONES

The country code for the US is 1 and should be dialed before any area code when using a landline. New York has five area codes: 212 and 646 for Manhattan; 917 mainly for cell phones, but also for Manhattan; 718 and 347 for the Bronx, Queens, Brooklyn, and Staten Island. Area codes are followed by a seven-digit number. For international calls, dial 011 + the country code + the number. Newsstands and drug stores sell calling cards for long-distance calls.

All numbers with an 800, 888, or 877 prefix are toll-free. You can dial directory assistance (411) for free from any phone.

Pay phones are scarce; you are better off buying a pre-paid cell phone SIM.

TIME ZONES

New York City is on Eastern Standard Time. In summer (between mid-March and early November), Daylight Saving Time is adopted, and clocks move ahead one hour. The time in various cities in winter:

Los Angeles	**New York**	London	Paris	Sydney
9am	**noon**	5pm	6pm	4am

TIPPING

Service is never Included in restaurant prices, but it is sometimes added to the bill when you are a group of six or more. In restaurants and bars, tip 15–20 percent of the total bill (New Yorkers traditionally double the sales tax). In general, porters are tipped $1–2 per bag; maids $1–2 per day; cloakroom attendants and doormen who find you a taxi, $1; taxi drivers and hairdressers, 15–20 percent. It's also expected to tip your server at a stand-up bar $1 per drink.

TOILETS

In general, the best facilities are those in the lobbies of major hotels or in department stores. Good bets in the Times Square area are the Marriott Marquis, and the generally well-maintained public toilets at nearby Bryant Park; in Lower Manhattan, the Museum of the American Indian, and Brookfield Place.

TOURIST INFORMATION

The Official NYC (www.nycgo.com) Information Center is inside **Macy's Herald Square** (151 W. 34th Street, Mon–Sat 10am–10pm, Sun 10am–9pm).

TRANSPORTATION (See also Airports)

Virtually every place that visitors are likely to go can be reached by public transportation. The basic fare is $2.75 (for bus or subway) one-way when you buy a **MetroCard**. Single fare tickets (when bought from the driver or vending machine) are $3. If you purchase a MetroCard, you can transfer between buses and subways for free. In addition to paying for each ride, you may buy an unlimited seven-day ($33) MetroCard. MetroCards can be purchased at all subway stations and at many drug and grocery stores and newsstands, including some supermarkets, and will be subject to a $1 fee. Bus and subway maps are available at major subway stations and transit hubs. For directions to reach any address in New York City by public transportation, tel: 511. See also www.mta.info.

Buses. All public buses are numbered and for Manhattan bear the prefix M (Q for Queens, B for Brooklyn, and Bx for the Bronx). Most either follow the avenues (except Park Avenue) or run cross-town along the major two-way arteries. They only accept the exact fare, or a MetroCard. Bus stops are indicated by a signpost showing a blue-and-white bus logo, and the bus number.

Subway. The network runs 24 hours a day, but not all entrances and token booths are open at all times. You may wish to avoid peak times (7–9.30am and 4.30–7pm). It is generally possible to make free transfers from one line to another at major transfer points. Local trains make every stop on the line; express trains do not. Lines are color-coded and identified by the last station on the line. Ensure you know the direction you are traveling in: *downtown* is southwards, *uptown* northwards. Despite occasional incidents, the subway is very safe: more than 5.5 million New Yorkers ride it every day, and on many lines in Manhattan, you'll see as many people on the train at 2am as you will at 2pm.

Commuter rail lines. The Long Island Rail Road provides rail service from Penn Station at 33rd Street and Seventh Avenue between Manhattan and Long Island (tel: 718-217 5477 or 511; www.new.mta.info/agency/long-island-rail-road). The Metro-North commuter railroad provides rail service between Manhattan and counties to the north of New York, including southwest Connecticut (tel: 511; www.new.mta.info/agency/metro-north-railroad). PATH trains go from 33rd Street and stops along Sixth Avenue or the World Trade Center to Hoboken, Jersey City, and Newark in New Jersey (fare is $2.75 using a Metrocard, tel: 800-234 7284; www.panynj.gov/path/en/index.html).

Taxis. Taxis are painted yellow and metered. If the light on top is lit, the cab is available. In Manhattan you can easily hail a taxi on the street, or go to a major hotel's taxi stand. Every taxi driver is expected to be able to speak English and to be able to take you to any address in New York City; they cannot legally refuse a fare if you are going to a destination within the city limits. The meter starts at $3.30 and increases by 50¢ every fifth of a mile (or 40¢ for waiting time). There is a 50¢ surcharge from 8pm–6am, a $1 surcharge for peak hours (4–8pm weekdays), plus the New York State Congestion Surcharge of $2.50. If your route comprises a toll tunnel or bridge, you must pay the toll. Taxi drivers will not accept bills higher than $20 and they generally expect a tip (about 15–20 percent or round up to the nearest dollar). They now accept credit cards for all fares. To complain about a driver, note his or her name and number and call 311. Such complaints are taken seriously.

Boro taxis. Introduced in 2013, apple-green Boro taxis operate in areas of New York not commonly served by yellow cabs: north of West 110th Street and East 96th Street in Manhattan, the Bronx, Queens (excluding the airports), Brooklyn and Staten Island. They can drop you off anywhere in the city, but are not allowed to pick up passengers in Manhattan below 110th/96th streets. Otherwise Boro taxis follow the same rules and fare structure as yellow cabs (and you can hail them on the street).

TRAVELERS WITH DISABILITIES

Most New York street corners are graded for wheelchairs. Buses can accommodate wheelchairs, though many subway stations are not accessible. Many hotels have rooms for guests with disabilities, but check when you make your reservation because some older establishments do not. The Mayor's Office for People with Disabilities (100 Gold Street, 2nd Floor, New York, NY 10038, tel: 311; www1.nyc.gov/site/mopd/index.page) can provide further details.

V

VISAS AND ENTRY REQUIREMENTS (See also Airports)

Canadians traveling by air must present a valid passport for entry. Visitors from the UK, Australia, New Zealand, and Ireland qualify for the visa waiver program, and therefore do not need a visa for stays of less than 90 days, as long as they have a valid 10-year machine-readable passport and a return ticket. However, they must apply online for authorization at least 72 hours before traveling at https://esta.cbp.dhs.gov/esta. There is an official processing fee of $4, and a further $10 authorization fee once the ESTA has been approved (all paid via credit card online). Citizens of South Africa need a visa. All foreign visitors have their two index fingers scanned and a digital photograph taken at the port of entry. The process takes only 10–15 seconds.

For the latest travel restrictions related to the Covid-19 pandemic, please check online at https://www.cdc.gov/coronavirus/2019-ncov/travelers/international-travel-during-covid19.html.

W

WEBSITES

The following websites will help you plan your trip:

www.citysearch.com/guide/newyork-ny-metro CitySearch

www.nycgo.com Official NYC Information Center

www.timeout.com/newyork events, bar and restaurant listings

www.mta.info regional transportation options

www.ny.eater.com reviews of the city's restaurants and eateries.

WEIGHTS AND MEASURES

The United States uses the Imperial system.

Y

YOUTH HOSTELS AND YMCAS (See also Accommodations)

The Hostelling International New York City Hostel is located at 891 Amsterdam Avenue, NY 10025 (tel: 212-932 2300; www.hihostels.com). Other hostels include the Chelsea International Hostel at 251 West 20th Street, NY 10011 (tel: 212-647 0010 www.chelseahostel.com); The Local NY in Queens at 13-02 44th Avenue, NY 11101 (tel: 347-738 5251; NY 11206 (tel: 347-227 8634; www.nymoorehostel.com); and Jazz on Columbus Circle Hostel at 940 8th Avenue, NY 10029 (tel: 646-876 9282; www.jazzhostels.com). Shared or dorm rooms start at around $42 per person in high season, with private rooms with shared bathrooms from $75.

There are also two YMCA where you can have a single or shared room with access to shared baths on a sex-segregated floor: the Vanderbilt YMCA, 224 East 47th Street, NYC 10017 (tel: 212-912 2500; www.ymcanyc.org/locations/vanderbilt-ymca); and the West Side YMCA, 5 West 63rd Street, NYC 10023 (tel: 212-912 2600; www.ymcanyc.org/locations/west-side-ymca). There are also YMCAs in Harlem, Flushing and Greenpoint (see website for details).

WHERE TO STAY

The only way to beat New York's notoriously high hotel rates is to come during the off-season (roughly Jan–Mar) or to get a package deal or weekend special. Advance reservations are essential most of the year. You will find the highest concentration of hotels in Midtown, between 42nd and 59th streets; others are in the 30s, both on the west side (near Herald Square) and on the east side (Murray Hill, including Gramercy Park). What you will not find here are most of the $500-plus luxury hotels.

Inquire direct about weekend specials; otherwise use one of the many online reservation services offering discounts of 50 percent or more on upscale rooms (www.kayak.com and www.hotels.com, to name a few).

The following categories apply to the cost of a standard or superior double room for one night and do not include tax of 14.75 percent plus $3.50 per night occupancy tax or the additional $25 (or more) "destination fee" changed by some hotels located close to Times Square. Unless otherwise indicated, rooms have private baths, direct-dial phones, cable television, and air-conditioning.

$$$$$	over $500
$$$$	$400–500
$$$	$300–400
$$	$200–300
$	below $200

DOWNTOWN

The Mercer $$$$$ *147 Mercer Street, NYC 10012, tel: 212-966 6060;* www.mercerhotel.com. A converted 1890s landmark building right in the heart of SoHo, the rooms feature high loft ceilings, arched windows, and (for New York) spacious bath facilities. Expect a stylish clientele and great food from the acclaimed Mercer Kitchen restaurant. 75 rooms.

Mr. C Seaport $$ *33 Peck Slip, NYC 10038, tel: 877-528 4249;* www.mrchotels.com/mrcseaport. A block from South Street Seaport, this converted 19th-century warehouse features contemporary, Italian-style rooms with all modern amenities. Children are well catered for with homemade cookies and milk provided on their first night. Some rooms on the upper floors have private terraces with views of the Brooklyn Bridge. 66 rooms.

Soho Grand Hotel $$$$ *310 West Broadway, NYC 10013, tel: 212-965 3000;* www.sohogrand.com. A sophisticated but comfortable hotel with all the high-tech and stylish amenities you might expect from an upscale hostelry that caters to the media and music-biz crowds. As befits a place owned by the heir to the Hartz Mountain pet empire, pets are welcome; for anyone who arrives without an animal companion, the management may be able to provide a complimentary bowl of goldfish. 353 rooms and suites.

Washington Square Hotel $$ *103 Waverly Place (MacDougal Street and 6th Avenue), NYC 10011, tel: 212-777 9515;* www.washingtonsquarehotel.com. This small, century-old, Art Deco hotel in Greenwich Village is one of the very few inexpensive options available downtown. Guest rooms, some of which look out over the park, are brightly decorated, and the restaurant, North Square, is one of the neighborhood's hidden secrets. 149 rooms.

MIDTOWN

1 Hotel Central Park $$$$$ *1414 Sixth Ave (at 58th Street), NYC 10019, tel: 212-369 1000;* www.1hotels.com. The eco-friendly hotel chain conceived by hotelier Barry Sternlich arrived here in 2015, with a three-story living wall, reclaimed rustic-chic furniture and everything organic, plus an on-call Tesla. In the luxurious rooms notepads are replaced by miniature chalkboards, and the clothing hangers are cardboard. 229 rooms.

The Algonquin Hotel $$$$$ *59 West 44th Street (5th and 6th avenues), NYC 10036, tel: 212-840 6800;* www.algonquinhotel.com. Close to Time Square, New York's oldest continuously operated hotel (it opened in 1902) and one of the city's famed literary hangouts has retained its old-club atmosphere (and famous house cat) from the days of the Round Table, though the rooms have been refurbished to handsome effect. Famous guests include Douglas Fairbanks, William Faulkner and Maya Angelou. Check out the legendary Blue Bar for a perfectly poured cocktail. 181 rooms.

The Benjamin $$$$ *125 East 50th Street (at Lexington Avenue), NYC 10022, tel: 212-715 2500 or 1866-222 2365;* www.thebenjamin.com. One of New York City's boutique-style hotels, the Benjamin offers business and leisure travelers four-star amenities and some of the most comfortable beds in New York, at relatively reasonable prices. Rooms have galley kitchens with a microwave and fridge, and some have terraces. There is also a spa, fitness center, restaurant, and cocktail lounge. The lovely Art Deco building was erected in 1927, the work of world-renowned architect Emery Roth. 209 rooms.

Casablanca Hotel $$$ *147 West 43rd Street (6th Avenue and Broadway), NYC 10036, tel: 212-869 1212;* www.casablancahotel.com. Wonderful, small hotels are rare in New York, yet here is a lovely and inviting choice. The décor throughout evokes Morocco, with Murano glass hallway sconces and beautifully tiled and appointed bathrooms. Continental breakfast included. 48 rooms.

Hotel Edison $$$ *228 West 47th Street (Broadway and 8th Avenue), NYC 10036, tel: 212-840 5000;* www.edisonhotelnyc.com. Though the Art Deco lobby can be chaotic, the rooms in this huge hotel are quite comfortable, pleasantly if simply decorated, and quiet. There is a large fitness center available. The complimentary walking tours are a good opportunity to learn about the neighbourhood. May be the best deal in NYC. 802 rooms.

Four Seasons Hotel New York $$$$$ *57 East 57th Street (Park and Madison avenues), NYC 10022, tel: 212-758 5700;* www.fourseasons.com. Arguably New York's best hotel, the Four Seasons has some of the largest rooms in the city (along with some of the highest prices). Elegant features include blond wood furnishings, bedside controls for everything, and separate showers and tubs. The lobby bar is also top-notch. 368 rooms.

The Iroquois $$$$ *49 West 44th Street (5th and 6th avenues), NYC 10036, tel: 212-840 3080 or 800-332-7220;* www.iroquoisny.com. This luxurious boutique hotel is close enough to the theater district to be convenient, but far enough away to be out of the path of most of the crowds. Standard rooms are not large, but they accommodate a king-size bed without feeling too cramped. The health club is first-rate. 114 rooms.

Mandarin Oriental $$$$$ *80 Columbus Circle, NYC 10023, tel: 212-805 8800;* www.mandarinoriental.com. Offering suites with beautiful views over Central Park and the rest of Manhattan, this five-star hotel provides not only a stunning setting, but also top of the notch service, comfort and style. There is also a spa, pool, glamorous cocktail bar, and celebrated restaurant. 248 rooms and suites.

Millennium Broadway $ *145 West 44th Street (6th Avenue and Broadway), NYC 10036, tel: 212-768 4400;* www.millenniumhotels.com. All of the rooms in this modern neoclassic tower are large and tastefully appointed, and all feature the usual business hotel amenities. 626 rooms and suites.

Paramount Hotel $$$$ *235 West 46th Street (8th Avenue and Broadway), NYC 10036, tel: 212-764 5500 or 844-881 5314;* www.nycparamount.com. A mix of retro and contemporary in the heart of Times Square. The rooms and public spaces pay homage to the theater design of the 1920s, but through a modern and minimalist lens. Amenities include extravagant 'entertainment suites,' access to the hotel's iPads and iMacs, and a classic theater district bar. Rooms are small but well equipped. 605 rooms.

Pod 51 Hotel $ *230 East 51st Street, NYC 10022, tel: 212-355 0300;* www.thepodhotel.com. This hotel will appeal to visitors on a budget looking for style and a dock for their iPhone. Rooms with bunk beds start at under $100 per night in low season. Rooms with a shared bath have in-room displays to indicate the availability of shared bathrooms. 348 rooms, including some with shared bath.

Sanctuary Hotel $$$ *132 West 47th Street (6th and 7th avenues), NYC 10036, tel: 212-234 7000 or 800-388 8988;* www.sanctuaryhotelnyc.com. Prices are reasonable, the style is hip and modern, and theater lovers will find the location ideal. 113 rooms.

The Shoreham $$$ *33 West 55th Street (5th and 6th avenues), NYC 10019, tel: 855-212 6773;* www.shorehamhotel.com. On a quiet residential street just around the corner from the Museum of Modern Art, this boutique hotel has a sleek, stylish lobby and bar. Rooms are fairly small but sumptuous and comfortable. 177 rooms.

St Regis $$$$$ *2 East 55th Street (at 5th Avenue), NYC 10022, tel: 212-753 4500;* www.marriott.com. Among the best of New York's palatial hotels, the St Regis is in the sweet spot of Fifth Avenue, right around the corner from MoMA and the most glittering shops. The Beaux Arts design is authentic from 1904. Rooms contrast high-tech amenities with French antiques; the King Cole Bar is famed for its Maxfield Parrish murals. 238 rooms.

HERALD SQUARE, MURRAY HILL, GRAMERCY PARK

Ace Hotel $$$$ *20 West 29th Street (at Broadway), NYC 10001, tel: 212-679 2222 or 212-991 0551;* www.acehotel.com/newyork. The hotel boasts a hip clientele, a celebrated restaurant and stylish rooms. At night, the lobby transforms into a club.

Hotel AKA NoMad $$$$ *131 Madison Avenue (at 31st Street), NYC 10016, tel: 212-448 7000;* www.stayaka.com/hotel-aka-nomad. This boutique hotel near Madison Square Park and the Flatiron Building, with a soaring lobby and soothing rooms, appeals to travelers who look for style with their room. The well-sized guest rooms make for a relaxing stay and an attractive choice in Murray Hill. Many rooms offer views of the Empire State Building. 194 rooms.

The Evelyn $$$ *7 East 27th Street (5th and Madison avenues), NYC 10016, tel: 212-545 8000;* www.theevelyn.com. A stylish boutique hotel in a red brick building right next to Madison Square Park. Rooms are beautifully decorated, with contemporary furnishings and wood floors have some luxurious touches. 160 rooms.

Hotel Giraffe $$$$ *365 Park Ave South (at East 26th Street), NYC 10016, tel: 212-685 7700;* www.hotelgiraffe.com. The tall and slender Hotel Giraffe contains rooms that invoke the sleek Art Moderne style of the 1920s and 1930s. Prices include complimentary breakfast, afternoon wine and cheese, and a 24hr espresso bar. 72 rooms and suites.

The Hotel @ New York City $$ *161 Lexington Avenue (at 30th Street), NYC 10016, tel: 212-545 1800;* www.thehotelatnewyorkcity.com. A lovely, small Murray Hill boutique hotel. It has a 24-hour fitness center and good restaurants nearby on Lexington Avenue. Continental breakfast included. 111 rooms.

IBEROSTAR 70 Park Avenue $ *70 Park Avenue (at 38th Street), NYC 10016, tel: 212-973 2400; www.iberostar.com.* This cheap and very popular chain hotel is adorned with original lighting and furnishing design featuring rich woods and pewter tones. Extras include 24hr fitness centre (and in-room spa services). Great deal. 205 rooms.

Kimpton Hotel Eventi $$$$ *851 Sixth Ave (at West 30th Street), NYC 10001, tel: 212-564 4567; www.hoteleventi.com.* Eventi is handily situated with good proximity to the Empire State Building and Madison Square Park. Patronized by all stripes, rooms are stylish without being overdone, and there's a tempting Italian restaurant (L'Amico), a knowledgeable staff and an excellent spa. 292 rooms.

Kixby Hotel $$$ *45 West 35th Street (5th and 6th avenues), NYC 10001, tel: 212-947 2500; www.kixby.com.* The lovely Art Deco lobby, with fresh flowers and leather chairs, is an oasis from gritty 35th Street. Guest rooms are fairly large and meticulously clean. The Lookup Rooftop bar offers spectacular views of the Empire State 195 rooms and suites.

Shelburne Hotel and Suites by Affinia $$$ *303 Lexington Avenue (at 37th Street), NYC 10016, tel: 212-689 5200; www.affinia.com/shelburne-hotel-suites.* With an eclectic, contemporary decor, the Shelburne, a member of the Affinia group, offers good-sized suites some with stunning views. Many suites have modern sleek kitchenettes and sofabeds. A good choice for families and business travelers. Fitness center. 325 rooms. Other Affinia hotels in New York include Fifty Hotel (155 East 50th Street, tel: 212-751 5710) with a fitness center and very reasonable rates.

The Tuscany $$$ *120 East 39th Street, NYC 10016, tel: 212-686 1600; www.stgileshotels.com.* This luxury boutique hotel is part of the St Giles chain of high-tech, upscale business hotels. The large rooms have all the trimmings you would expect at these prices, including free Wi-Fi, data ports and dual-line phones. 124 rooms and suites.

THE UPPER EAST SIDE

Sherry-Netherland $$$$$ *781 Fifth Avenue, (at East 59th Street), NYC 10022, tel: 212-355 2800; www.sherrynetherland.com.* One of New York's most luxurious hotels – the stunning views of Central Park are worth the exorbitant cost alone. Dating from 1927, the lobby is modeled after the Vatican Library and splendidly ornate; service is excellent and room service is by the in-house Harry Cipriani restaurant. 50 rooms.

voco The Franklin New York $$ *164 East 87th Street (3rd and Lexington avenues), NYC 10128, tel: 212-369 1000;* www.franklinhotel.com. The old-fashioned exterior of the Franklin doesn't prepare you for the elegant and stylish modern rooms inside. Though not large, all the modern details have been well thought out, and the human scale of the place and the hotel's friendly staff are definite pluses. Convenient to the subway and Fifth Avenue museums. 50 rooms.

THE UPPER WEST SIDE

Arthouse Hotel New York City $$ *2178 Broadway at W 77th Street, NY C10024, tel: 212-362-1100;* www.arthousehotelnyc.com. Chic and modern hotel with great views over the city. Features a lively Prohibition-era-inspired bar as well as two restaurants to choose from. The hotel also frequently hosts art exhibitions with the likes of Jean-Michel Basquiat and Andy Warhol gracing the walls. 291 rooms.

Hotel Beacon $$ *2130 Broadway (at 75th Street), NYC 10023, tel: 212-787 1100 or 800-572 4949;* www.beaconhotel.com. An apartment building converted into a hotel. The good news for travelers is that a cramped New York apartment makes a spacious hotel room, and every room has either a king bed or two double beds and fully equipped kitchenettes. Convenient for the Beacon Theater, Lincoln Center, Natural History Museum, and Central Park. More than 270 rooms.

Lucerne Hotel $$$ *201 West 79th Street, NYC 10024, tel: 212-875 1000 or 800-492 8122;* www.thelucernehotel.com. Housed in the beautifully renovated 1904 building, this boutique hotel boasts elegantly furnished comfortable rooms. Some suites include kitchenettes. Spa services, 24-hour room service, and fitness center are available as well as the restaurant, Nice Matin. 202 rooms and suites.

INDEX

9/11 memorial 25
30 Rockefeller Center
    (Comcast Building) 39

A

accommodation 116
Africa Center 55
airports 116
AMC Empire 36
American Academy of Arts
    and Letters 67
American Folk Art
    Museum 61
American Museum of
    Natural History 62
American Museum of the
    Moving Image 83
Apollo Theater 66
Audubon Terrace 67

B

Battery Park 26, 27
Battery Park City 25
Bedford Street 74
Belvedere Castle 59
Bethesda Terrace and
    Fountain 58
Bowling Green 27
Bronx 80
Bronx Zoo 81
Brooklyn Botanic Garden
    80
Brooklyn Bridge 33
Brooklyn Heights 79
Brooklyn Museum 79
Bryant Park 37

C

Carnegie Hall 36
Carousel 57
car rental/hire 119
Castle Clinton 26
Central Park 55
Channel Gardens 39
Chelsea Piers 78
Chinatown 71
Christopher Street 75
Chrysler Building 45
Circle Line 37
Cleopatra's Needle 59
Columbia University 65
Columbus Circle 59
Conservatory Garden 59
Conservatory Water 58
Cooper-Hewitt,
    Smithsonian Design
    Museum 54
Covid-19 11, 124, 131
crime and safety 120
customs regulations 121

D

Daily News Building 45
David Geffen Hall 61
David H. Koch Theater 61
Delacorte Theater 59
disabilities, travellers
    with131
Dyckman Farmhouse
    Museum 69

E

East Village 75

Ellis Island 29
El Museo del Barrio 55
embassies and consulates
    122
Empire State Building 46
ESPN Zone 36
E-Walk 36

F

Father Duffy Square 36
Federal Hall National
    Memorial 32
Fifth Avenue 40
Ford Foundation 45
Fort Tryon Park 68
Fraunces Tavern 30

G

General Post Office 48
Grand Army Plaza 41
Grand Central Terminal 44
Grant's Tomb 65
Great Lawn 59
Greenwich Village 73

H

Hamilton Grange National
    Memorial 67
Hamilton Heights 67
Harlem Meer 59
Hayden Planetarium 63
health and medical care
    124
High Line 76
Hispanic Society of
    America 67

I

Intrepid Sea, Air & Space
Museum 37

J

Jacob K. Javits Convention
Center 48
Jacqueline Kennedy
Onassis Reservoir 59
Jewish Museum 55
Joyce Theater 78

L

Lever House 44
LGBTQ+ 74
Lincoln Center for the
Performing Arts 60
lost property 125
Lotte New York Palace
Hotel 43
Lower East Side Tenement
Museum 70

M

Macy's 47
Madame Tussaud's Wax
Museum 36
Madison Square Garden 47
maps 125
Metropolitan Museum of
Art 51
Metropolitan Opera
House 60
MoMA PS1 83
Morgan Library & Museum
48
Morris-Jumel Mansion 67
Mount Vernon Hotel
Museum and Garden 49

Museum of Arts and
Design 60
Museum of Chinese in
America 71
Museum of Jewish
Heritage 26
Museum of Modern Art
(MoMA) 42
Museum of the City of
New York 55

N

National Museum of the
American Indian 27
NBC Experience 40
Neue Galerie 53
New Museum 71
New Victory Theater 36
New York Botanical
Garden 82
New York City Hall 33
New York Historical
Society 62
New York Public Library 38
New York Stock Exchange
32
New York Times Building
37
New York Transit Museum
79
New York University 74
Noguchi Museum 83
North Meadow 59

O

Old Customs House 27
One World Trade Center 25
Orchard Street 69
Oyster Bar & Restaurant 44

P

Pierre 41
Plaza 41
police 127
Police Headquarters 72
Port Authority of New
York 37
post offices 127
Promenade 79
Prospect Park 80
public holidays 127

R

Radio City Music Hall 40
Rockefeller Center 38

S

Schomburg Center for
Research in Black
Culture 67
Seagram Building 44
Shearith Israel Cemetery 71
Sheep Meadow 57
Soho 72
Solomon R. Guggenheim
Museum 53
South Street Seaport 33
South Street Seaport
Museum 33
Statue of Liberty 28
statue of Prometheus 39
St Mark's-in-the-Bowery 76
St Nicholas Historic
District 66
Stone Street 30
Stonewall 75
St Patrick's Cathedral 41
St Paul's Chapel 32
Strawberry Fields 58

T

Tavern on the Green 57
The Cloisters 68
The Public Theater 75
The Studio Museum in
    Harlem 66
Times Square 34
Tisch Children's Zoo 57
Titanic Memorial
    Lighthouse 33
Top of the Rock 39

Tribeca 73

U

United Nations 46

V

visas and entry
    requirements 131
Vivian Beaumont Theater
    61

W

Waldorf-Astoria Hotel 44
Wall Street 31
Washington Heights 68
Washington Square
    Park 74
Whitney Museum of
    American Art 77
Winter Garden 26
Wollman Rink 57
Woolworth Building 33

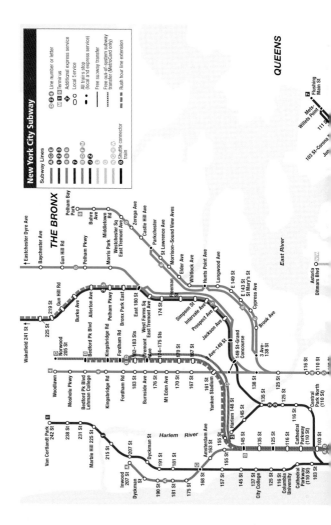

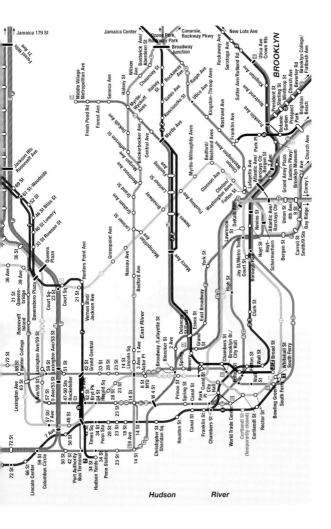

THE **MINI** ROUGH GUIDE TO
NEW YORK

First Edition 2022

Editor: Beth Williams
Author: Stephen Keeling
Picture Editor: Tom Smyth
Cartography Update: Carte
Layout: Pradeep Thapliyal
Head of DTP and Pre-Press: Katie Bennett
Head of Publishing: Kate Drynan
Photography Credits: Abe Nowitz/Apa
Publications 39, 56, 61, 62, 64, 67, 76, 78; Britta
Jaschinski/Apa Publications 27, 30, 31, 40, 42,
54, 58, 60, 87, 89, 91, 94, 97; Getty Images 12, 17;
iStock 5M, 7T, 19, 63, 74, 80, 81, 84, 92, 103, 104;
Keiko Niwa/Lower East Side Tenement Museum
70; Marley White/NYC & Co 11; Public domain
14, 52; Richard Nowitz/Apa Publications 36, 72,
73; Shutterstock 1, 4TC, 4MC, 4MC, 4TC, 4ML,
4TL, 4ML, 5T, 5M, 6T, 6B, 7B, 26, 32, 35, 41, 43,
44, 46, 47, 48, 50, 82, 101, 106; Tagger Yancey IV/
NYC & Company 22; The Metropolitan Museum
of Art 69
Cover Credits: Central Park and Midtown
Manhattan **TierneyMJ/Shutterstock**

Distribution
UK, Ireland and Europe: Apa Publications (UK)
Ltd; sales@roughguides.com
United States and Canada: Ingram Publisher
Services; ips@ingramcontent.com
Australia and New Zealand: Booktopia;
retailer@booktopia.com.au
Worldwide: Apa Publications (UK) Ltd;
sales@roughguides.com

**Special Sales, Content Licensing
and CoPublishing**
Rough Guides can be purchased in bulk
quantities at discounted prices. We can create
special editions, personalised jackets and
corporate imprints tailored to your needs. sales@
roughguides.com; http://roughguides.com

Contact us
Every effort has been made to provide accurate
information in this publication, but changes
are inevitable. The publisher cannot be held
responsible for any resulting loss, inconvenience
or injury sustained by any traveller as a result
of information or advice contained in the
guide. We would appreciate it if readers would
call our attention to any errors or outdated
information, or if you feel we've left something
out. Please send your comments with the subject
line "Rough Guide Mini New York Update" to
mail@uk.roughguides.com.